D1760485

The Practical Specifier

LIBRARY
MIDLANDS TECHNICAL COLLEGE
BELTLINE CAMPUS

The Practical Specifier

A Manual of Construction Documentation for Architects

Walter Rosenfeld, AIA, CSI

McGraw-Hill Book Company

New York St. Louis San Francisco Auckland Bogotá
Hamburg Johannesburg London Madrid Mexico
Montreal New Delhi Panama Paris São Paulo
Singapore Sydney Tokyo Toronto

TH
425
.R63
1985

Library of Congress Cataloging in Publication Data

Rosenfeld, Walter.
The practical specifier.

Includes index.
1. Building—Contracts and specifications. I. Title.
TH425.R63 1985 692 84-15396
ISBN 0-07-053779-8

38417

Copyright © 1985 by McGraw-Hill, Inc. All rights reserved. Printed in the United States of America. Except as permitted under the United States Copyright Act of 1976, no part of this publication may be reproduced or distributed in any form or by any means, or stored in a data base or retrieval system, without the prior written permission of the publisher.

Chapters 1–4, 6–15, 17–21, 23, 24, 26, and 27 are not covered by this copyright. Chapters 1, 3, 4, 6, 7, 9–11, 13–15, 17–21, 23, 24, 26, and 27 originally appeared in *Progressive Architecture* magazine. Chapters 2, 8, and 12 originally appeared in the *Construction Specifier*.

1234567890 DOC/DOC 8987654

ISBN 0-07-053779-8

The editors for this book were Joan Zseleczky and Dennis Gleason, the designer was Dennis Sharkey, and the production supervisor was Teresa F. Leaden. It was set in Electra by Achorn Graphics. Printed and bound by R. R. Donnelley & Sons, Inc.

contents

List of Illustrations

preface

There is no apparent shortage of written material dealing with specifications. Professional association publications, manuals of practice, reference works, and copyable model specification sections are widely distributed and available to beginners and experienced specifiers alike.

The Construction Specifications Institute and several technical and professional schools provide courses in different parts of the country which emphasize the basic techniques and outline the scope of the specifier's work. Even the master specifications sections of CSI (*Spectext*) and the American Institute of Architects (*Masterspec*) have instructions to specifiers built in to them.

No end of literature and instruction supports the specifier's continuing education throughout his or her years of practice. Mind and mailbox are continually filled with data from manufacturers, catalogs, magazine articles, monographs, seminars, conferences, and product shows.

Add to this influx of technical literature the specifiers' need to be currently informed about and understand the legal implications for their work of contract law, construction law and practice, contract conditions, methods of bidding, government regulations, and so on. It's no wonder that a whole sector of industry has thrived on this educational effort.

Still, in spite of great quantities of published material, most of the specifier's training is typically done on the job, in professional offices. And much of the learning is through observing, listening to, and working with experienced practitioners who are willing to share their knowledge and to try to develop skills in the novice so that their own work loads can be lightened, their responsibilities shared, and their firms helped to prosper. Doing it daily and over long periods of apprenticeship is the basic and probably the best way of becoming proficient at specifying, assuming inclination, latent ability, and reasonable background are there. Experience is a good teacher, though a time-consuming one, but it needs supplementing with thought about the work being done, study and research, and continuing feedback with the results of one's efforts.

For in the end, specifiers are largely self-taught and continue to teach themselves throughout their careers. Because it is through doing, experiencing, and learning that skills and understanding are developed, an "experienced specifier" is what one tries to become, even knowing that experience is always relative and incomplete for any one person. Long after the in-house teachers are gone and specifiers are on their own, the real world continues with its lessons. The necessity of learning fast and learning well is accelerated by the demands of construction, the argument of lawyers, the pressure of owners. To head off the mistakes of others is the specifiers' job; to head off their own mistakes is their urgent need.

To help specifiers at any stage of their careers by looking at some situations that are not addressed extensively in specifications literature is the purpose of this book. For the more experienced architect or engineer who may have faced some of these subjects already, it is my hope that the book will bring back to mind important issues often forgotten. For the less experienced, I hope the book will open up new areas for constructive thought and suggest new solutions to recurrent problems. For those early in their careers, I hope it will indicate some basic directions to take and how to apply knowledge learned from others. For all those working on specifications, the book is intended to be a practical help in their daily professional lives as they analyze projects, produce contract documents, meet deadlines, and make their essential contribution to construction in our own country and around the world.

The Practical Specifier is divided into three main parts. Part 1 deals with the basic task of producing the project manual. Part 2 explores the context in which the specifier works and the industry of which he or she is a part. Part 3 concerns itself with the specifier's role in the process and with problems not always directly related to getting the documents out. Part 4 contains the appendixes.

Since the architects, owners, specifiers, manufacturers' representatives, consultants, contractors, and others one meets in building construction activities today may be either men or women, I have tried to omit gender-specific terminology from this book wherever possible. If, through inadvertence or oversight, some vestige of obsolete assumptions remains undetected, I hope it can be forgiven and pointed out for correction in any future edition.

Most of the chapters are based on articles which have appeared in *Progressive Architecture* or in *The Construction Specifier* over the last several years. I want especially to thank Peter Moore, Publisher of P/A and Gene Dutchak of CSI for their gracious permission to use this material.

I also want to express my appreciation to Richard Rush AIA, former Technical Editor of P/A for his help and encouragement; to the late Hugh MacFarlane and Ken Litaker CSI, who got me into specifying; to Ron Chiaramonte CSI and my many other colleagues at The Architects Collaborative for sharing problems and solutions with me over the years; to Joan Rogers, Ellen Hakim-Johnson, and Lisa Almeda for their typing and word processing help; and finally to my wife, Marilyn, to whom this book is dedicated.

Walter Rosenfeld

The Practical Specifier

part 1

The Project Manual

chapter

1

Formulating Master Outline Specifications

Since an outline specification is often required to accompany design development phase drawings for presentation to an owner, a funding agency, or a contractor estimating the probable cost of the work, having a master outline specification ready for adaptation to the project at hand is clearly a great convenience. While some funding agencies have "outline specifications" available to be filled in for a particular job and may even require their use, in most cases these are inadequate to describe the intended results for architectural work, and the architect must provide something more appropriate.

If the outline specification follows the trade-oriented Construction Specification Institute's (CSI) sixteen-division organization of material, it will not only make pricing easier but will also enable the document to serve later on as a basis for the project manual to be written along similar lines during the working drawings phase. Using a master outline to produce the job outline has two further advantages: it requires necessary materials decisions to be made more systematically at this time, and, more importantly, if properly set up, the master can be used as a checklist of decisions to be made or items to be included in the work. This latter function is quite consistent with a basic principle of writing any kind of master section: to include the most frequently required items and options and to edit chiefly by deleting unwanted material. The best masters therefore will aim to minimize time-consuming research and the writing of new material.

To set up a master outline specification, a brief section format should be established, along with a flexible numbering system which allows easy insertion and removal of items as well as providing for the contributions of consultants to be inserted or added later on. Either the alphanumeric American Institute of Architects' "(AIA) system" or the all-digit "CSI system" will work, but thought should be given to making the document adaptable to word processing or other electronic storage and retrieval, either now or in the future.

The search for source material for the master outline specification should start with the office master specification, if there is one. Ideally, the best master outline is a distillation of the firm's standard master specifications. Lacking an office master, the next best sources are project manuals for major projects with large numbers of materials and applications, taken apart and sorted by section. Use of such in-house material gives continuity and predictability to future outlines and permits the incorporation of materials and construction policies developed by the firm during its previous history. If the firm is using a commercially available master specification such as *Spectext* or *Masterspec,* these sections should be reviewed as well. So far, producers of master specifications have not themselves provided master outline specifications along these lines for use by their subscribers.

Begin by preparing short stock minisections for each trade and material, paring the complete reference sections down to essential information. Use short declarative and imperative sentences to identify the materials to be used and the important characteristics of their installation. In most cases, the "General" portion (Part 1) of a typical complete section can be omitted entirely.

While such minisections should fully establish all the basic materials of a building, they ought particularly to concentrate on items which affect cost and those which are important to the architectural character of a building. However, specifying details of construction should generally be avoided.

The master outline will include more sections than any real building would ever require. For example, both conventional and inverted built-up roofs; steel, aluminum, and wood windows; and a variety of exterior wall systems may all be described if the firm's buildings are likely to use them. Where sections or items are mutually exclusive, they can be identically numbered to alert a future editor to choices which must be made.

Materials and methods can be specified by reference to American Society for Testing and Materials (ASTM) or American National Standards Institute (ANSI) numbers, by description of the product, by performance requirements, or by manufacturer's name and model number. Some items will indicate the scope of work; others will just list essential requirements for each trade. To simplify things, groups of related items can be gathered into one minisection such as Building Specialties and given as little as one line each, even though later on each may have its own section in the final project manual.

Examining each reference section and condensing the significant information into a collection of such minisections is the major task in setting up master outline specifications. Once completed, however, the document should well repay the effort in convenience, consistency, and speed.

chapter

2

Setting Bid Dates and Times

Architects and specifiers charged with preparing contract documents for public or private bidding are often called upon to set the time and place for distribution of these documents and for receipt of bids, all in the course of their regular work. Ordinarily this is a simple decision-making procedure and is done without much hesitation. However, changing of bid dates and times occurs frequently enough to indicate lack of forethought in some cases and unawareness of many consequences of bid-timing decisions in others. Extraordinary cases may always arise, but planning professions should certainly be able to anticipate most of the usual problems. Here are some ideas which may help in making such decisions.

When to Go Out

Does it really matter what day of the week or what time of day bidders are invited to pick up documents for bidding? It usually does.

A major consideration is the logistics of printing the drawings and specifications. Offset or other reproduction of a project manual containing 300 pages, together with collating and binding, is not generally an overnight operation (and if it can be done overnight, overtime pay rates usually apply). Therefore, unless the specifications are ready for the printer several days in advance, reproduction may hold things up.

From this it logically follows that Monday morning at 8:30 A.M. is not a good time to promise documents unless the job can afford double-time pay in exchange for the printer's Sunday. In fact, Monday, with its high incidence of holidays and absentee problems (not to mention the four-day work week), cannot be considered a good day for issuing documents in any but the most unusual cases.

A word might also be said about Friday. Printing problems are not severe here, but the likelihood of contractors picking up documents late Friday afternoon is slim. Even if they do have the materials, few work over the weekend.

Since drawings can usually be printed in small quantities and with less advance notice, specification printing time generally governs.

Recommendations: Issue documents Tuesday through Thursday, after lunch (2:00 P.M.) for an extra safety margin, or, if you must, before noon on Friday. Watch out for holidays and long weekends when setting dates.

Advertising

Another factor to consider is the length of time required for prior advertising, often a statutory requirement in public bidding, and the infrequency with which some local newspapers are issued. If advertising copy for a weekly paper that comes out on Tuesday must be submitted the preceding Thursday, the bid advertisement will have to meet the paper's deadline and precede the issuance of documents by the required interval when it appears in print. Generally, newspapers will not accept legal advertising over the telephone, and of course the advertisement cannot be written until the bid dates have been set.

Where to Pick Up Documents

It is important that the place chosen for distribution of documents be selected carefully, for its facilities and availability of people to do the job properly. Front office personnel at such a place must be familiar with bidding problems and procedures.

Perhaps the most important activity in connection with distributing documents is keeping the records of the whereabouts of each set of drawings and specifications. Unless there is an accurate listing of all bidders who have taken out plans, serious problems, often with legal consequences, may arise when addenda must be distributed. To aid the architect, it is often useful to keep this list in terms of whether the bidder is a general contractor or whether the bidder represents a specific trade. Listing of bidders by trade is essential where filing of subbids or separate prime contracts are required by law.

Usually the architect's office is able to handle document distribution, but many times the location of the building site, and consequently of the prospective bidders, is far enough away to make distribution of documents by the architect impracticable. In this case it is especially important to brief the local person responsible, preferably in writing, and to maintain close contact with him or her during the bidding period. If no such person is available, the place is not suitable for distributing documents. Handling and safely storing plan deposit checks also requires special instruction and security provisions. Municipal, state, and institutional clients are usually equipped to carry out these procedures.

When to Receive Bids

Since contractors will be receiving figures and information from suppliers and subcontractors until almost the hour that bids are due, the ideal bid-opening time is toward the end of the working day. In fact, many general contractors have indicated support for evening bid openings, a practice which has worked well when the owner is a school committee that normally meets in the evening. Evening bid openings give general contractors some time to analyze and arrange their figures after all their subcontractors and suppliers have closed shop for the day. This does not always suit the owner's convenience, however, and in some cases the time for opening bids is set by statute and must be adhered to lest the whole bidding be declared invalid.

Common bid-opening times are 2:00, 3:00, or 4:00 P.M., and these seem to meet most practical requirements. Evening openings are generally scheduled for 8:00 P.M.

Monday and Friday are again the least recommended days. Monday holidays and absences aside, Monday openings present a very short work day for bid preparation. Friday again runs into early-start weekends. For the same reasons, days after holidays should be avoided. Tuesday, Wednesday, and Thursday seem most satisfactory.

Where to Open Bids

Three considerations shape this decision. First, hall capacity should be sufficient to accommodate the anticipated attendance. Good acoustics and some comfort for the participants are important, too. Second, accessibility and parking facilities should be adequate for the inevitable last-minute inrush of bidders. Sensibly, most bidders send both a driver and a messenger to turn in bids in case parking is unavailable. Nevertheless, late arrivals can pose legal and other problems. Thirdly, clerical personnel must be available at the bid-opening site who can receive, time-stamp, and protect the envelopes, without opening them, and who know enough to hand them unopened to the responsible master of ceremonies at the proper moment.

An additional desirable and often important convenience at the place of bid opening is availability of public telephones so that bidders can contact their offices to check on final prices and last-minute changes.

Also important is someone to collect and preserve bid bonds, checks, and bid forms after the opening in a secure fireproof place until the bid security is returned and the contract awarded and signed.

Sometimes the architect's office has these facilities and people. Often the owner has them. Every effort should be made to find a place that has them all.

Length of Bidding Period

Bidders obviously need sufficient time after obtaining documents to study them, determine quantities and types of materials needed, and to get prices from subcontractors and suppliers. A reasonable period of time for this activity to take place effectively is the main determinant of the length of the bidding period. There are, however, other factors to consider.

Quite frequently addenda to the documents must be issued to clarify conflicts and obscurities, and sometimes to effect changes in scope or conditions of work. Serious errors affecting prices can also occur during preparation of the contract documents, and if the bidding period established is not long enough to allow corrections by addendum, the period may have to be extended, However, changing bid dates should be avoided if at all possible because it easily leads to confusion, misunderstanding, and unforeseen conflicts. Usually someone affected does not "get the word" in time. In anticipation of addenda, bid documents should state the cutoff date for receiving questions, preferably in writing, and not less than one week before bids are due. This allows the specifier or architect time to write and type the addendum; others time to review it; the printer time to print, punch, and collate it; and the postal service time to get it into the bidders' hands.

Sufficient time must therefore be allowed during the bidding period for information to be collected from all parties, owner, architect, consultants, contractors, suppliers, approval agencies, and others; for this material to be sorted, coordinated, typed, and printed; for addenda to be mailed or otherwise distributed; and for addenda to be received by bidders enough in advance of the bid due date so that they can make adjustments; determine new quantities, materials, and requirements; obtain revised prices; and still submit the bid on time.

Actual processing of addenda usually requires the preparation of many envelopes and labels and the time-consuming registering or certifying of mail. People and time must be assigned for this work as well, and the amount of time will vary with the procedures and personnel of each office.

Unfortunately, feedback and questions from bidders generally come in only at the last minute, when their full attention is finally concentrated on the job just before the deadline. In many cases questions arrive too late to be answered in written addenda properly distributed to all. Thus the bidders are forced to "use their best judgment" regarding the information on hand in the existing contract documents and tend to pad their bids accordingly. It is absolutely necessary for addenda to be in written form. Verbal or telephone changes and explanations should be strictly avoided as they only lead to later trouble and disturb the intended equality of all bidders' information.

The minimum time period for competitive bidding should therefore be at least two weeks, but most jobs require longer. International work may need as much as ninety days or more. Most small jobs require three to four weeks at current activity rates, and larger work a month to six weeks. As has been indicated above, a too-short bidding period can lead to higher bid prices of itself by causing hurried contractors to cover the uncertainties they have not had time to analyze or price by increasing their bids. A too-long period can disperse interest in the work or unduly delay the beginning of construction.

Consultation with prospective contractors on the amount of time they would like is often helpful before setting dates and will also reveal the existence of other work on which these contractors are bidding at about the same time. Jobs attractive to the same group of contractors should not be bid unintentionally at the same time from different offices or both jobs will suffer, either through fewer bidders or less precise pricing.

Time and Price

Given the firmly established status of competitive bidding, it becomes clearly important for architects, owners, and specifiers to develop an understanding of contractors' practices and problems and to set bid times and places with these considerations in mind.

Proper timing and placing of the activities of all members of the construction team encourages vigorous and honest bidding. Both owner and contractor can thereby more easily arrive at an agreement which allows the proper construction of the proposed building at the best possible price.

chapter

3

Writing Consultants' Specifications

One of the specifier's major responsibilities is to organize the project manual for each building. In addition to working out a table of contents, the specifier needs to establish details of the document's format, including page layout, job identification, paragraph numbering system, and typeface, among others. Decisions, not necessarily difficult ones (Do we underline? What words are capitalized?) have to be made, whether or not the CSI section format is used, and these decisions have to be communicated to everyone involved. A look at entries in the annual CSI specifications competition indicates that there are still many ways of putting together a project manual and that each way has its own rules.

More important, the specifier must coordinate the work of all trades and establish the responsibilities of each within a common contractual framework. Which trade will provide access panels for mechanical equipment? In what form does the architect want shop drawings submitted? Who is responsible for temporary electricity? Such things must be determined at an early stage and written into the different sections to which they apply.

But in actual practice, many sections of a typical project manual are written by people other than the specifier in charge. Consultants to the architect may prepare as many as half the pages of the manual (or more) and may be responsible for specifying more than half the cost of the work. As a result, the specifier always faces the problem of how to get consultants to write their sections so that the desired final product is achieved: a project manual consistent in form and content, uniform in appearance, and without conflict in instructions to its users. Ideally, all parts of the document should fit together as though they were written by one person and typed on one typewriter.

Against this need for consistency and uniformity is the consultants' tendency to have different writing styles, organizational notions, paragraphing systems, technical requirements for submissions, and their natural desire to do all of their specifications the same way on every job. Consultants are often tempted, too, to use their last specification as a basic document, whatever that job was, however it was bid, wherever it was located, and whoever the client or architect was. Or they may want to use their computer-based master sections, even though the format may be totally different and difficult to adapt.

One way specifiers can deal with these problems is to write (and type) consultants' specification sections for them, at least the first few pages (Part 1 of the three-part section format), in draft form, and to turn these pages over to the consultant along with a brief memo on the style rules to be observed in the remainder of the sections. These documents can be distributed at an early team meeting or by mail, but persistent follow-up is usually required for enforcement. If the architect has computer capability, this part of each consultant's section can be prepared by editing existing masters.

There is no real question here of taking on the consultants' responsibilities or liabilities, since no technical specifications are written for them; only procedural and contractual items are dealt with, and consultants have the opportunity to review and revise these as may be required. But once consultants receive this draft, many essential decisions are clear and they can proceed to write their technical specifications directly, having in front of them a good example of the required format, the chosen numbering system, the correct page layout, the applicable job identification, and even the selected typeface. The goal of visual uniformity is much closer.

With this sample in hand, consultants are also alerted to such things as related work under other sections (for coordination), any limitations of scope, and the special clauses often required by institutional owners or governmental funding agencies. References to the general conditions or general requirements of Division 1, which incorporate a unified system of dealing with shop drawings, record drawings, submittals, substitutions, project closeout, and so on, are established, and the need for each consultant to repeat them, often with unwelcome variations, is eliminated. Consequently, the goal of consistent procedure and coordinated work is more easily achieved.

Since by this method all the basic coordinating information for each consultant's trade is concisely conveyed (the medium being part of the message), a more consistent and complete project manual should result, no matter who writes a particular section. Confusion during bidding should therefore be significantly reduced and avoidable conflicts prevented as the project moves on into construction.

chapter

4

The Well-Begun Project Manual

You have a shelf full of master sections, a library full of manufacturers' literature, a box full of recent specifications by others, the CSI *Manual of Practice* is on your desk, and it's time to prepare the project manual for a new building. When do you start and what do you do first? Is there a logical sequence to this work that actually helps? Yes, there is.

Begin by determining the type of contract you are writing (or are there multiple contracts?). Will the work be done for a fixed lump sum or for construction cost plus a fee? Is there a construction manager? Do the rules of a government agency establish the general conditions? Remember that whoever is paying for the building will have a say about the way the contract is set up and the documents to be used. Last, will the project be bid (under some of these same rules, perhaps) and require bid forms for soliciting prices? To start specifying without these questions answered is to risk redoing technical sections as well as bidding and contract forms, because the entire project manual is affected by them. With the answers known, bidding requirements, contract forms, and general conditions can be prepared with confidence, no matter what stage the drawings are in.

Next, examine the available drawings to determine what trades are involved in this construction. List the materials indicated and make shrewd guesses about others that may be required. Organize the trades according to the CSI *Masterformat* and make a rough table of contents. Now you begin to have a notion of the work before you: how many sections need to be written and what information will have to be assembled.

The third step, an important one, is to organize the specifications work of consultants and others contributing to the project manual. Though several professionals are writing this book in collaboration, the ideal is to have it all appear to have come from the same writer (consistency of style) and from the same typewriter (consistency of format). For this purpose, a brief memo to consultants and page format samples are useful, as indicated in the previous chapter. But more is needed if everyone is to be oriented to the same rules.

Not only do the format, numbering system, paragraphing, page identification, and typeface have to be established for everyone, but certain technical arrangements have to be worked out as well. How will access panels be handled? Who will provide temporary services? How will testing be paid for? The work must be divided clearly among the trades without duplications or omissions. Does everyone know the rules for bidding alternates? Will all specify the same guarantee period? Will all handle shop drawings the same way? Though the work is done in parts, it must eventually fit together as one document. Providing Part 1 of such sections is a practical way of handling these problems.

Now you are ready to begin the architectural sections, but where should you actually start? Since the specifications are a record of decisions about materials and construction methods for each job, it's best to start where the fewest decisions need to be made or where all the necessary decisions have already been made. Therefore, it's often not very productive to start technical sections before working drawings are about 50 percent complete unless you have unusually good information about what materials will be used. By that time, a number of sections can usually be started from the information already on paper.

For example, you might start with Section 10160, Toilet Compartments, because comparatively few decisions are required. Do you want metal or plastic laminate units? Are they floor-mounted or ceiling-hung? Are there urinal screens or special features? With very little more than the answers to these few questions, the entire sections can be written; the remainder is relatively standard. For each project there is a group of sections requiring a minimum of decisions, and they are generally the first to be written.

As the drawings progress, you can proceed to other areas. If the door and finish schedules are done early, additional sections can follow. Wall sections and details should be drawn before window and roofing specifications are written. Glass types must be decided before glazing can be done. Toward the end you can tackle sections which need many details, or sections which require extensive consulting with sales representatives or specialists before writing begins.

While working to complete the sections on your list, don't lose sight of the basic goal: to set down precisely what is wanted, so that bidders know what to price, so that owners know what they are getting, and so that the architect can properly control the result; in short, so that the building that is wanted is the one that is actually built.

chapter

5

Bookkeeping

The first step in producing technical sections for the project manual is usually modifying or editing section masters that already exist in hard-copy form or are held electronically.

To make this first pass or draft, the specifier reviews progress drawings, consults with the architect, the project team, and others about the work of one trade or section. He or she also reviews current product literature and talks to manufacturers' representatives if necessary.

The section master specification is then edited to suit the project requirements, is checked for format as well as contents, is given the job title or identification to appear in each page heading (or footing), is dated perhaps, and then . . . then what?

The section is either stored electronically or printed out as a progress copy, or both. Since sections are produced sequentially (by whatever means), they accumulate over the period during which the specifier is working on the project. Ideally they're perfect and need only be collected, printed, and bound, ready to be handed over to the bidders.

But that seldom happens. In fact there are usually numbers of changes to each section as the work is completed on the drawing boards and more detailed decisions are made which affect various trades. Materials are often added and must be specified, or materials are deleted. Additional coordination items arise and consultants' specifications arrive to be worked into the project manual.

With the aid of electronic equipment, making the changes is not overly burdensome. But keeping track of the changes still poses practical problems, and having one up-to-date version of what has been done or decided so far can be very helpful. The advent of electronic media has not always made this easier, since many hands often have access to the keyboard.

One traditional but very effective way of handling this problem is to provide two hard-copy prints of each section as it is completed. One copy should go to the project architect and the other should be kept by the specifier. A pair of loose-leaf notebooks in which to collect the sections is handy. As changes are worked out, they are recorded by the specifier in one copy. Notes about needed changes are made by the project architect in the other copy as he or she reviews what the specifier has done and compares it with newer drawings and as-yet-unrecorded intentions.

Except under duress (a client or agency review, for example) more draft copies incorporating changes are *not* made as the work progresses, but notes are merely added to the first draft and held until the end of the documentation period. Then architect and specifier get together, go through their annotated versions of the project manual, complete the changes, and record them all in the specifier's copy which becomes the correct final version for updating the original just before printing.

In this way the plague of too many progress sets (or lack of a permanent reference set) is avoided; decisions are recorded in a timely and effective way at only two locations; and the final reconciliation is simple. In addition, the architect becomes familiar with the project manual as it is being produced and has an opportunity to participate in assuring its completeness and accuracy. Of course there are occasions when this procedure can't be followed and date stamps must be used to try to keep the (printed) records straight, but as a standard procedure it has many advantages to recommend it.

chapter

6

From Manufacturer's Data into Specifications

As part of their sales programs, manufacturers of construction products have always provided descriptive literature and product data to inform prospective users of the characteristics and virtues of their materials. Traditionally, specifiers have relied heavily on such literature in preparing specifications for building projects. Before the days of industrywide master specifications, "writing from scratch," using these kinds of data, was the norm for both new materials and new applications of familiar materials and took a lot of the specifier's time and energy.

The trouble with most manufacturers' handouts and catalog information in those days was usually their sales orientation. Limitations on use were seldom indicated, and needed technical data were often omitted. Incomplete or missing installation information frequently presented problems, and the data each manufacturer chose to supply were often different from those of competitors, which made comparison of characteristics, construction, and performance quite difficult. No general standards for format or content of manufacturers' literature existed until CSI introduced *Spec-Data* to deal with the situation.

In the words of James Sigel, manager of this very successful program, "*Spec-Data* is a product bulletin, condensed to eliminate extraneous materials and promotional language. All data are arranged into ten standard categories: product name, manufacturer, description, technical data, installation, availability and costs, guarantee, maintenance, technical services and filing systems. This standard arrangement aids product comparisons and locating specific information." While use of *Spec-Data* sheets reduces the time needed for research and telephone calls to manufacturers when transforming product information into specifications, a great deal of "writing from scratch" is still required because of the way the data are structured.

Can more be done to speed the process? The next logical step beyond *Spec-Data* has already been taken. Under the CSI *Manu-Spec* program, the manufacturer drafts a sample specification for the specifier's use. As Sigel puts it, "*Manu-Spec* is a prepared specification section written in the CSI three-part format, but for a manufacturer's specific product. It shows the way a manufacturer's product should be specified." Thus a *Manu-Spec* for a chosen product can be rather easily transformed into a narrow-scope section for a particular project manual or incorporated into a broader-scope section which includes it among other products.

Is this the end of specifying as we have known it? Hardly. For among the things neither CSI nor the manufacturer can do for us is to choose the appropriate products for the project and to decide what characteristics we want in the products we select. Frequently one product alone is not enough for a competitive situation where the contractor, too, must be given a chance to choose. And of course, each project has its own requirements and rules, to which the specifications must be adapted.

While a large number and a great variety of products are covered by *Spec-Data*, fewer *Manu-Specs* have been written so far. One hopes this program will also prosper and multiply. But for product groups and processes not completely covered by either *Spec-Data* or *Manu-Spec*, CSI does offer another service—the Technical Aids Series (TAS) which describes the resources, documents, and information available to the researcher of building components and materials. Each TAS document covers one category and lists all applicable standards and regulations, available specification aids (such as those mentioned above), institute and association publications, related books and periodicals, and all known manufacturers. It is a complete bibliography of the essential information needed to prepare a specification, and is thus of great time-saving value.

But no matter what form product information may take, the specifier still has to get the project manual organized and written and must make sure that the appropriate products are properly specified and closely coordinated. When resource materials don't have the answer, the specifier must still consult directly with manufacturers' representatives to get the needed information. And in spite of all the documentary help available, specifiers surprisingly often still find products, applications, and variations that are not adequately described, that still require writing new descriptions, new instructions, or new sections on many of their projects from scratch.

Even today, turning project information into specifications continues to be one of the basic activities of the specifier. It's a lot easier now because of CSI-sponsored documents, but it still requires experience, skill, and good judgment, as all specifying does.

chapter

7

Barrier-Free Specifications

Only recently have specifiers begun to realize some of the far-reaching implications of making buildings more accessible to the physically handicapped. Though ANSI A-117.1 has been in existence over two decades (revised again in 1980) and forms the basis of efforts to standardize architectural approaches to such problems, it is only within the last few years that federal and state governments have begun to respond with new code requirements which affect both private and public buildings. In any case, the need to alter existing buildings and to change our thinking about new buildings, often in subtle ways, to provide barrier-free access and use is now clearly established in law and practice.

While the specifier will follow the architect's lead in code compliance, as indicated on the contract drawings, many essentials can only be handled in the specifications. Though the drawings show locations, delineate details, and indicate quantities (or schedule them), the sources and characteristics of materials and most performance requirements can best be described in the project manual.

For example, not only the height and locations of grab bars in toilet rooms are needed ("see drawings") but also their diameter, surface texture, and secure attachment ("as specified"). A type of mirror mounting that tilts downward for wheelchair-bound users may be necessary. Out-swinging toilet compartment doors will need unconventional hardware. Such items are more economically specified rather than illustrated and noted in great detail.

The examples above are taken from only one division of the project manual, but meeting requirements for barrier-free buildings is not limited to one division nor is it a single section or division itself. Rather, it requires a series of items and changes in a large number of trade sections spread throughout the contract documents. In fact, almost every division is affected by some code or construction provision.

While a list of items in each division (from drain grates which do not trap wheelchairs in Division 2, through lever handles or blades on faucets in Division 15) can be compiled, the majority of items are concentrated in three general categories: travel, convenience facilities, and communication.

Travel is the broadest group, since access is a prime goal. It includes textured, nonslip ramp surfaces; substantial hand and guardrails; automatic door openers; door closers not requiring excessive pull to operate; hardware with lever handles; knurled door knobs at hazardous areas; low thresholds and saddles for minimum obstruction; and substantial kickplates to protect door finishes.

Also included in the travel category are low-pile carpet which won't impede wheelchair progress, nonslip floor coverings, nontrip stairs without projecting nosings, flush edges where floor finishes change or terminate, platform lifts and elevators with proper features, braille or raised numbers at elevator car and hall stations, self-leveling elevators, and adequate door-open time for elevators. Audible arrival gongs help the visually impaired.

In addition to the toilet items already cited, the convenience facilities category includes secure attachment for towel bars which may become emergency grab bars, omission of curbs and steps at showers, kitchen ranges with door swings that don't obstruct the wheelchair user from reaching into the oven without danger, front controls on drinking fountains, insulation of exposed hot undersink pipes, and hand showers with flexible hoses.

"Communication" means adequate indication of facilities such as special wide parking spaces; building signs and graphics to show ramp and other access locations; oversize lettering and color coding of areas; audible signals (as at elevators); and doorless, acoustically treated telephone booths, some at wheelchair height, with special equipment for the hearing impaired.

Review of the typical items mentioned above will show that Sitework, Concrete, Masonry, Miscellaneous Metals, Carpentry, Doors and Hardware, Finishes, Specialties, Equipment, Conveying Systems, and Mechanical work are all affected. Furnishings and Special Construction sections may also be involved in a particular project. If we add to Division 1 a general statement of intent to provide accessibility (sometimes required by a funding agency), very few divisions of the project manual remain untouched.

It may be surprising at first to realize the extensive effect of these new requirements on specifications work and the wide variety of handicaps intended to be accommodated. The barrier-free specification, however, is not merely an exercise in code compliance. It is an attempt to make available to disadvantaged groups the conveniences and experiences that the rest of the population routinely enjoys. As such, it calls for the specifier's humane sympathy and conscientious effort.

chapter

8

Some Practical Aspects of Time Clauses

Specification writers and owners over the years have tried various means to incorporate into construction documents clauses of sufficient strength to bind contractors to specific, mutually acceptable completion dates for projects. Because such efforts have by no means always resulted in unqualified success, new approaches are constantly being sought and tried.

There are today three widely used approaches to the problem of insuring building occupancy dates: the essential condition, liquidated damages, and progress of work clauses. Each has certain merits as well as limitations, and from time to time, all three appear in the same contract.

Essential Condition Clause

The essential condition clause may be typified as follows:

> It is hereby understood and mutually agreed, by and between the Contractor and the Owner, that the date of beginning and the time for completion as specified in the contract of the work to be done hereunder are ESSENTIAL CONDITIONS of this contract; and it is further mutually understood and agreed that the work embraced in this contract shall be commenced on a date to be specified in the "Notice To Proceed".
>
> The Contractor agrees that said work shall be prosecuted regularly, diligently and uninterruptedly at such a rate of progress as will insure full completion thereof within the time specified. It is expressly understood and agreed, by and between the Contractor and the Owner, that the time for the completion of the work described herein is a reasonable time for the completion of the same, taking into consideration the average climatic range and usual industrial conditions prevailing in this locality.

This clause, written into the agreement as well as into the special conditions of the contract, makes failure to complete the work by the specified date grounds for a suit for breach of contract. That such suits are not frequent occurrences in the courts, considering the vast amount of construction activity, may be attributed to several factors.

First, because it involves a failure to complete work begun and carried on, a breach of contract usually occurs when the work is well advanced, and in many cases, nearly complete. Having on hand a nearly complete building, the owner tends to be concerned not primarily with the legal recourse available but with the most expedient method of getting the building completed.

Depending on the amount of work remaining to be done, the reasons for the delay, and the financial condition and the attitude of the contractor, the owner's best course often is to press for completion as soon as possible, using the threat rather than the reality of court action as a weapon. The goodwill and the willing cooperation of the delinquent contractor are the true essential conditions for the speedy and economical completion of the building, and neither will be improved by forcing the contractor to defend in court the conduct of the construction operation up to the time of breach. The owner has the further recourse of withholding payments, beyond the customary 10 percent retainage, in the knowledge that breach of contract entitles the contractor to no further payment. The contractor will therefore become aware that the best chance of getting paid is the speedy completion of the work.

It is assumed here, of course, that both parties intend the full performance of the contract. For, if the contractor is unable or unwilling to complete the work beyond the deadline, it must be taken over by the owner and administered by the owner or the owner's agent, usually the architect, at additional expense to both. Should the owner then file a breach of contract suit under this essential condition clause, the work would most likely be halted for a further period while legal counsel and clarification were sought. For these reasons, therefore, action under this provision of the contract serves more as a last resort than as a ready course of action.

The matter is further complicated by the existence of Article 8.3, "Delays and Extension of Time," in the frequently used AIA General Conditions (Document A201),

> If the Contractor is delayed at any time in the progress of the Work by any act or neglect of the Owner or the Architect, or by any employee of either, or by any separate contractor employed by the Owner, or by changes ordered in the Work, or by labor disputes, fire, unusual delay in transportation, adverse weather conditions not reasonably anticipatable, unavoidable casualties or any other causes beyond the Contractor's control, or by delay authorized by the Owner pending arbitration, or by any other cause which the Architect determines may justify the delay, then the Contract Time shall be extended by Change Order for such reasonable time as the Architect may determine.

And Article 8.3 includes the additional provision:

This paragraph 8.3 does not exclude the recovery of damages for delay by either party under other provisions of the Contract Documents.

The building that proceeds without change orders, without any possible justification for delay under this article, is indeed the exception rather than the rule. Even if the original period allotted for construction is more than adequate (also seldom the case), justifiable delays often occur, and others of a more dubious nature will be construed as justifiable and will be so used by the shrewd contractor who has any anticipation of failing to complete on time.

The very possibility of justifiable delay in construction, however, strikes at the heart of the essential condition clause, for so very likely are these delays to occur, that they render unlikely the completion of the building on the specified date. Therefore, in order to make this provision fully compelling and to place the entire and absolute burden on the contractor to complete on or before the required date, it would appear necessary to delete Article 8.3 from the General Conditions in its entirety. Of course, any contractor who was aware of such an omission would be forced to increase the bid price accordingly to cover the increased risks, or might decline to bid the job at all under these conditions.

Liquidated Damages Clause

The extreme nature of the essential condition approach, requiring for its application a complete break in the building operation, has led to the use of a more moderate clause requiring payment of "liquidated damages" by the contractor subsequent to failure to complete. The contractor in this case still remains in charge of the construction, and in the usual case, the contractor's loss is small compared to what might be lost under a breach of contract suit. The legality of such clauses has been tested in the Supreme Court (*U.S. v. United Engineering and*

Contracting Co. 234 US235, 58 L ed 1294) and are in common use. A typical liquidated damages clause might read as follows:

The Contractor agrees to substantially complete the building on or before the date specified in the Agreement, or before the date determined by the Architect under the provisions of Article 8.3.

In the case the work is not completed within the time specified in the Agreement, or within the time allowed by the Architect under Article 8.3 of the General Conditions, it is hereby understood and agreed that the Contractor shall pay to the Owner, not as a penalty but as liquidated damages, the sum of $100.00 (one hundred dollars) for each and every calendar day after and exclusive of the day within which completion was required, up to and including the date of substantial completion of the work, said sum being agreed upon as the measure of damages to the Owner by reason of delay in the completion of the work. Such damages shall be deducted from the contract price, and the Contractor shall agree and consent that the contract price, reduced by the aggregate of damages so deducted, shall be accepted in full satisfaction of all work done under the contract.

Two difficulties are encountered in the use of this clause, both having to do with setting the actual amount of damages to be required. The actual damages suffered by reason of failure to complete in time may be very difficult or impossible to determine. Where they can be determined, they should of course be used. However, such sums as would constitute penalties have been ruled unenforceable by the courts under common law. Fixing the precise sum is therefore critical as well as difficult, and in practice, the amount is necessarily related to the amount of the contract.

In a large contract of, say, $10 million, for a building to be constructed over a period of two years, with a critical completion date, the sum of $500 per day might not seem excessive. The length of time after the completion date required to extinguish the total contract price in damages would still be quite long in relation to the time allotted for construction. However, the amount involved is substantial enough to encourage the contractor to exploit every possible justification for delay in the course of the work under Article 8, and the result is usually a barrage of correspondence to the architect alleging unavoidable delays beyond the contractor's control in matters of supply, labor, owner's actions, architect's tardiness in returning shop drawings, making decisions, solving problems, coordinating work, and processing change orders.

Architect's acts causing delay under Article 8 are usually the chief content of such a delay justification file, and any "act or neglect," from not immediately furnishing drawings to failure to be in the office when the contractor telephones, prompts a letter claiming this as a factor in the prolongation of the construction period. In the course of two years, these items can generally be counted on to furnish enough justification for delay as to make the exercise of the liquidated damages clause a remote likelihood. In addition, these items cause architects so much additional paperwork that they are often reluctant to write this large an amount into the contract.

An additional factor may be the owner's urgent need for the building. Contractors have often used this need to their advantage by threatening delay as a means to extract larger prices for change orders and extra work. The work usually has to be done at the contractor's price, no matter how inflated it may be, if the building is to be completed on time. The extra profit in such negotiated items can go a long way to offset any liquidated damages the contractor may eventually be required to pay the owner.

On the other hand, if the amount stipulated for liquidated damages is nominal, say $100 a day on a $2 million contract to run one year, the contractor may discount it entirely. A few change orders at negotiated prices, inflated by the contractor as indicated above, will take care of several months of damages. The smaller amount is often used, however, in the hope that the mere existence of such a clause, while not calling forth the amount of correspondence that the maximum would draw, may yet have the effect of cautioning the contractor that the owner is in earnest about the date of completion. Because it is more nominal, this amount is more likely to be given up by the contractor and collected by the owner, especially in the event the owner is a public authority that can to some extent satisfy taxpayers, irritated at the delay, with the answer that the contractor has paid for the delinquency in the amount the public records show.

In practice, however, the collection of such liquidated damages does not seem to be common, and the owner either ignores the clause or bargains it away in exchange for some other advantage.

The other side of the damages coin is the bonus provision, which, even considering its infrequent use, has a somewhat better record. If the money is available and the urgency is great enough to warrant the expense, a substantial bonus is more likely to encourage early or timely completion than any other means of exerting pressure. The contractor will often willingly work overtime and exert considerable effort to finish early if the stakes are set high enough. The obvious disadvantage of the method, that it is inherently costly, is usually an overriding factor, however, especially in the case of public work. In addition, most owners feel that the loss possible from failure to complete is likely to be less than the more certain payment of a bonus high enough to be effective. Another disadvantage is that public officials are often apprehensive that the use of a bonus clause may invite charges of collusion against them alleging that they have arranged excessive time for completion and expect a kickback or other favors from the contractor who does the work and gets the bonus.

Progress of Work Clause

A third approach to the time factor in building construction contracts has been less direct. Rather than (or in addition to) stipulating financial considerations in the case of failure to meet the deadline, many contracts are written with clauses requiring contractors to submit progress schedules at the beginning of the job, and having made the schedules themselves, requiring strict adherence to them thereafter.

> Within five days after the General Bidder selected as the General Contractor has received a "Notice to Proceed," he shall prepare and submit to the Architect a progress schedule for the entire work. Said schedule, after being approved by the Architect, shall be strictly adhered to during the course of the work, and failure to comply with said schedule, except as provided in Article 8.3, shall be deemed sufficient cause for the Architect to withhold certificates of payment.

This type of clause is often introduced as a modification of the last paragraph in Article 4.10 of the AIA General Conditions, which is far less compelling:

> The Contractor immediately after being awarded the Contract shall prepare and submit for the Owner's and Architect's information an estimated progress schedule for the Work. The progress schedule shall be related to the entire project to the extent required by the Contract Documents, and shall provide for expeditious and practicable executing of the Work.

More modest in intention than the other types of time clauses, the progress schedule provision is regularly used and reasonably successful, but in a less stringent manner. The schedule is an outline of the contractor's work, and the contractor will generally stick to it as closely as possible, not out of apprehension, but out of convenience. There is not much question here of legally fixing a rigid termination-of-work date, but the owner will get the building as soon as the contractor can get it done, considering the various delays that might be encountered. This is not to say that the progress schedule has no value. On the contrary, it is essential, but it cannot give more than a rough indication of when the completed building will be available for occupancy, and this is often less certain than the owner would wish. In situations requiring a specified completion date, the progress schedule clause is insufficient when used alone.

A more recent version of the traditional progress schedule requirement is the attempt to write into the contract a requirement that the progress schedule be done in terms of a critical path diagram, which more precisely schedules the work around certain critical dates in the construction schedule, including the beginning and end of work. The chief advantage of the critical path diagram seems to be its graphic presentation of the course of construction, making evident the dependence of certain activities on others, and on the whole job's being represented in terms of the interdependence of related activities, each of which must be completed in the time span allotted. It also tends to include all the trades and events, some of which may be left out of the more traditional progress schedule by inadvertence or carelessness.

The initial impression of completeness and absoluteness of the diagram is mitigated by the realization that it is subject to revision or updating as often as every two weeks, and that the revisions take into account the delay or incompleteness in one or more paths or activities.

A contract clause substituting a critical path diagram for the progress schedule of Article 4.10 would be enforceable under the same terms, chiefly Article 9.6, as the progress of work clause quoted above, and would read similarly with appropriate additions and substitutions.

Contractors have shown considerable acceptance of the diagrammatic method and many favor it themselves as an aid in the planning and coordination of their work. That it can have the compelling legal force of essential condition or liquidated damages clauses is not expected even by its proponents. However, it does offer the prospect of a guide under which the "regular, diligent and uninterrupted prosecution of the work" may be accomplished, and it does indicate the rate of progress which "will insure full completion thereof within the time specified."

chapter

9

Seven Sins of Specifying

"Thou shalt not" might be too strong a way to preface these recommendations on what to avoid when specifying, but consider the consequences carefully before getting into any of the situations discussed in this chapter.

1. Misdirecting Instructions

Since the sixteen-division uniform construction index which forms the basis of the project manual is fundamentally trade-oriented, it is important to keep in mind that each section has its own specialized audience: the trade which does the specified type of work. Although the general conditions may insist that the work is an indivisible whole, there is considerable evidence that each trade reads just those technical sections applicable to itself. Therefore, the specifier should address a trade only in its own section and not somewhere else, however related two activities may seem.

If certain wood trim will be varnished rather than painted, you can say so in the millwork section, but don't go into varnish materials and application there if another trade is going to apply the finish. Of course you must then be sure to include varnish work in the painting section. A "related work" paragraph in each section can be used for coordination.

Drawing a line between trades is sometimes difficult and often demands special knowledge. Trade members can help clarify jurisdictions, but where doubt exists it's usually better to assign the work to someone (if you want it included in a bid) rather than to ignore the problem.

2. Cold Copying

Without reviewing a reference document for applicability to the project at hand, it is not possible to prepare a competent specification. Whether the reference is an old specification that has been used successfully before, a master from the office file or from a specification service, a manufacturer's draft, or even an industry standard from ASTM or ANSI, don't copy it or incorporate it by reference into your project manual without checking to be sure exactly what it says.

The old office section or master may have obsolete or inappropriate parts. *Spectext* and *Masterspec* are regularly updated and changed. What appears to be a performance specification from a manufacturer may actually be proprietary and exclusive. ASTM periodically revises its standards too.

Unless you've looked at it recently, you may find surprises in a once-familiar reference. Are there choices to be made regarding finishes, optional items, performance categories? The person who takes responsibility for the specifications needs to know what's included and what isn't. You can't be sure if you haven't read it through.

3. Pinpointing

Using the project manual to locate the precise spot in the building where a specified material or product occurs generally causes problems. The item may also be needed in another location not mentioned. Or it may be deleted later from one place and not another. In each case, the specifier has to go back and make changes which might have been avoided. The burden of changes is much increased by this troublesome practice and occasions for error are multiplied.

More important, perhaps, pinpointing violates the necessary division of documentation between drawings and specifications (CSI *Manual of Practice,* MP 1–7, "Relating Drawings and Specifications") under which the drawings show locations, dimensions, and relationship of materials, and the specifications describe the materials' characteristics and methods of installation. If pinpointing were carried out to a logical conclusion, the drawings would barely be needed and the project manual enormous and awkward. This doesn't mean that you shouldn't schedule toilet accessories or light fixtures or describe locations in a general way or for typical situations. It does mean that specific locations should be left to the drawings unless there is a compelling reason to do otherwise.

4. Potpourri

Since sections of the typical project manual come from several sources for final assembly at the time of printing, it is not likely that there will be much coherence, uniformity, or consistency to the finished product unless the specifier makes a substantial effort to organize, coordinate, and set standards for all the contributors. Failure to do so may result in conflicting requirements for shop drawings, guarantees, temporary facilities, and other job procedures, as well as duplication of work and incorrect or inadequate assignment of work to trades.

Such failure can also lead to the visual chaos in which each section has a different appearance, typeface, page format, numbering system, and (even) job identification. Conflicts and confusion tend to result in higher job costs for the architect as well as the contractor (and therefore the owner) so that this sin is not merely one of cosmetics, but of substance. Aside from errors and omissions, coordination failure is probably the largest single cause of avoidable job extras. High priority should be given to coordinating all work included in the project manual.

5. Puzzle Making

Specifiers sometimes amuse each other by citing passages they've come across in (other writers') project manuals. Aside from finding hilarious typographical errors (now alas far fewer with automated document production), a favorite pastime is reading aloud a paragraph which no one can understand, often followed by the comment, "I wonder what they actually built." Surely one of the greatest sins of specifying is writing something incomprehensible to the likely reader.

The questions "What does this mean?" or "What do they want me to do?" signal the specifier's failure to communicate his or her intention. The CSI *Manual of Practice* provides a good review of some basic principles of clear writing in MP-1–10, "Specifications Language," which should be followed. When using established text, word changes carefully. When preparing new text, ask someone else to read it over for verification that it means to others what it means to you.

Fancy rhetoric, elaborate phrase making, long and awkward sentences have no place in this practical, legal document, the project manual. Use simple declarative and imperative statements. Write less rather than more. Don't abbreviate. Don't repeat. Finish what you start. Set things up in a logical sequence so that there is a path for the reader to follow. Use standard technical and trade language, but not slang (it may turn out to be ambiguous or unclear when they read it in court). And, if you haven't seen the process you're describing, try to find someone who has written it up from eyewitness familiarity.

6. Fiction Writing

Of course it's possible to write clearly and still be in trouble if you're specifying something you can't have or can't get. You can't have concrete cast to watchmaker's tolerances on your building. You can't pick and choose features from different manufacturers' window products and specify them all in one unit unless you are willing to accept the great cost of a custom product, if indeed it can be manufactured at all.

Since specified products are purchased in an ever-changing marketplace, specifiers have to know what is available and what is possible in that marketplace in order to do their work properly. They need to know the costs of what they specify as well as the owner's reasonable budget for the building. They need to know how products are designed, manufactured, and fabricated and must specify realistically within the limits of each trade. The specifier's judgment and advice in these areas are valuable to the architect in making materials decisions, but they must be based on economic and production realities.

Someone has to find, price, buy, fabricate, ship, and install everything specified. If any of these steps can't be accomplished, the building process may be interrupted; and the burden of that interruption may fall on the specifier or the ultimate client, the owner.

7. Taking Over

When preparing the project manual, it is important to keep in mind the separate roles of the architect and the contractor under the standard form of agreement (AIA A101 or A111) and the general conditions of the contract (AIA A201). Under A201 Article 4.3.1, the contractor (not the architect) is responsible for the conduct of the work. There are times when the architect is tempted to tell the contractor how to do things that are (or should be) the contractor's responsibility: forms of fire protection during construction, how to erect staging or scaffolding, and the like. Such temptation should be resisted.

Design of the building to comply with OSHA and other legal requirements is the architect's duty. Seeing that the job site complies is the contractor's. Specifying the safety result you want to obtain is generally proper. Specifying the method by which the contractor is to achieve the result may not be wise: "Comply with applicable Occupational Safety and Health Administration requirements," yes; "Build guardrails around all openings 2′-6″ high with posts 3′-0″ on centers" is risky, even where technically correct.

The architect who assumes (by so specifying) responsibilities that under the contract belong to others may not only be liable for unfavorable results but may even find that professional liability insurance offers no protection in some cases. Don't take over the contractor's work; there's enough for the architect to do in his own role.

chapter

10

American Specifications for Overseas Work

Despite unsettled world conditions and lack of specific government support, American architects continue to design a great deal of work overseas, particularly in developing countries whose own architects are few or are just beginning to get established in practice.

Aside from learning different systems of documentation and coping with import restrictions and currency fluctuations, a significant amount of the architect's time is devoted to obtaining information about local materials and methods of construction and to deciding what materials to specify under a variety of building conditions.

Matters are often complicated by requirements to

specify (or not to specify) materials from certain other nations for traditional or political reasons, but it is clearly true that an immense variety of products from all over the world can be made available today for a construction project wherever it may be. What then is a reasonable policy for American architects to adopt when specifying materials for overseas work?

If the country where the building is to be constructed has a well-developed set of national standards, whether indigenous or borrowed, the task is simplified; but the specifier must first become familiar with a whole range of documents—usually complex, sometimes expensive, and often difficult to obtain.

Where such systems exist, specifications can be very brief and of the performance type, with reference to the established standard for the material or method of installation. And where locally produced materials are suitable, they are, of course, the logical first choice. In other cases, however, proprietary foreign products need to be specified, and this presents two problems.

First, a country's products are usually produced to that country's own standards. In the United States, structural steel conforms to ASTM A-36; in Britain to BS-4360; in France to NF A35-501; and these standards are by no means identical. While some industrial countries produce materials to foreign standards in order to widen their markets, if materials are specified to British standards, the specifier is encouraging (at least) or demanding (at most) that British-made products be used.

Second, in international bidding, it is often impossible to know in advance the nationality of the contractor who will build the building. Experience indicates that contractors will tend to buy products from familiar sources with whom they have established lines of credit, most likely in their own countries or trading areas.

It makes little sense, therefore, on any one project, to specify some products from Japan, some from Germany, some from Britain (even though the architect may become familiar with such products), because what the specifier picks from France, the contractor may intend to buy in Sweden or Italy. Since the as-yet-unidentified contractor can't be outguessed, the best course is to produce a consistent range of products against which the contractor's choices may be measured. A program for evaluating and dealing with substitutions is therefore necessary, and the contract documents should indicate that the architect is prepared to do this. In any case, it is advisable to list several manufacturers for each product, together with their addresses and telex numbers.

It does make sense, however, for American architects to specify American products and American standards for overseas work in any case where an alternative approach is not mandatory. This is a practical (rather than patriotic) policy for many reasons. A substantially complete selection of American-made products is available from diverse sources in the United States; a competitive pricing situation exists for most materials; active export effort and capacity are evident; and abundant technical information and assistance are at hand. Unfortunately, relatively few overseas manufacturers provide as good a level of product information as can be found in *Spec-Data* sheets and similar United States' literature. Too, the architect practicing in the United States over a number of years knows which American products and manufacturers are reliable and proven in service under a variety of conditions. The manufacturers' accessibility at the architect's home location and the absence of language barriers are additional inducements.

Unless the owner insists on limiting what is specified to those items currently marketed in the country where the building is located (from whatever national origin), American standards and materials should generally be acceptable as a basis for bidding and for actual use. The architect's natural first inclination to specify American products for overseas work need not always be resisted in the name of uncertainty. In fact, careful analysis of the situation may reveal it to be a very sensible policy after all.

chapter

11

Some Afterthoughts about Addenda

Like the other contract documents, addenda serve several functions between the bidding period and building occupancy, and they are used differently by a variety of participants in the building process at different times. This variety of functions and users is important in determining the form as well as the content of addenda and significantly influences the characteristics of addenda in common use.

"Addenda are written or graphic instruments that are issued prior to the opening of bids which clarify, revise, add to, or delete from the original construction documents of previous addenda," according to MP-1–8 "Changes to Bidding and Contract Documents" of the CSI *Manual of Practice.* The architect issues addenda "to correct errors or omissions in drawings and specifications, clarify questions raised by bidders, or issue new requirements, including decisions to decrease or increase the scope of certain work."

During the bidding phase, addenda are addressed primarily to bidders and subbidders who need the additional information in order to prepare their bids, but suppliers also check addenda for changes in material requirements. While the owner's lawyers and funding agency officials examine each document for changes which may affect bidding procedures, the architect's consultants, often major contributors themselves to addenda, review proposed items to help coordinate their work. The effect of these needs during bidding is to require separate binding of each addendum for distribution to those who already have the other contract documents, and, perhaps, punching of holes in the addendum to facilitate insertion into their project manuals. Drawing and specification changes need careful separation, and the arrangement of items in page-by-page and drawing-by-drawing sequence serves to aid users in locating items.

Although addenda are issued to revise the original documents before the contract is awarded, they are far from obsolete once bids are received. As the emphasis turns toward construction, new users appear on the scene and previous users take on new roles. Their interests must be anticipated so that the document will be most useful during the construction phase.

Clearly, the contractor, subcontractors, and suppliers continue to need the information the addenda contain in order to carry out their new contractual obligations; so do the project representative and the job supervision staff from the architect's office. Reviewing addendum items is particularly important when checking shop drawings and manufacturers' data once the work has begun. Then, too, should contention arise, the various parties' lawyers will examine these same items again.

Cross-referencing of addenda to the original documents by page-turning is far less convenient than the common practice of most users in the field: posting the changes where they occur in the earlier documents. Consequently, addenda are often cut apart and portions pasted on the page or drawing where they apply, and where they are less likely to be overlooked or lost. For this reason it is good practice to use colored paper for addenda, making the items stand out when posted. And, of course, while the original project manual may be printed on both sides of the page to save space and weight, addenda are never done that way, since one-side printing is essential for cutting and posting. Another good practice is to attach a newly issued specification section to the addendum as an appendix rather than incorporating it as an item in sequence. Now the specification section can be separated out and inserted as a whole in its proper location in the project manual, integrated into the working document, even though issued late.

If the several addenda are each printed on a different color paper, identification of the source or timing of any item becomes easier, since some of the parties will still be working from the bound addenda while others will have theirs already posted. In an arbitration or court proceeding, for example, an addendum would be introduced as a complete, unaltered document; while at the job site, the contractor's and the architect's copies will be pasted up early on.

The *Manual of Practice* concedes that "In practice, changes constitute a relatively small percentage of the work, especially considering the number of possible errors, omissions, additions, changes of mind, and updating of methods or materials that could influence the course of construction." While automation of production may decrease the number of specification errors and thus minimize the size of a typical addendum, the necessary speed with which contract documents are often produced almost guarantees the persistence of the addendum as a tool for dealing with the inevitable changes. Thinking about the multipurpose nature of the document and its various users will help in preparing more successful and usable addenda whenever they are needed.

part

The Context 2

chapter

12

Specifications in the Spectrum of Style

Automation of specifications production has by no means ended the need for clear writing and explicit instruction on the part of those who prepare project manuals for construction contracts. On the contrary, the need has never been greater for owners, specifiers, and contractors to understand each other well in this era of high construction costs, accelerated time schedules, and costly litigation.

From its early days, CSI has knowingly included chapters on specifications language in its *Manual of Practice*, and sessions on writing in its professional practice seminars. The current document, MP-1-10, "Specifications Language" (1980), deals with the rudiments of sentence structure, the proper use of "shall" and "will" (what the contractor is to do as opposed to what the owner or the architect is to do), the importance of the imperative, or command, mode in contract documents, and other such elements of good language usage.

Similarly, lectures and workshops sponsored by CSI deal with the same basic subjects and refer to various writing handbooks in an effort to improve the specifier's written language skills. An early course at New York University some fifteen years ago sponsored by CSI's New York chapter became a model when its outline was circulated to those producing similar seminars across the country. The NYU instructor, Charles DiPierro, included in his notes the somewhat cryptic line which forms the title of this chapter, and it remains years later to puzzle many would-be instructors who never attended his seminar.

Even so, the suggestion that there is a place for specifications writing as writing amongst humanity's literary accomplishments holds the power to inspire the writer's best efforts along with the tendency to pique his or her curiosity as to where it all fits in.

Where are specifications in the "spectrum of style?" What have specifications to do with poetry, fiction, and drama? We know that the project manual has two connected aspects: it is, at the same time, a legal and a technical document. Most specifying is technical writing of a special kind that has the legal character of a contract between an owner and a contractor. Even the most "legal" parts, the general and special conditions, have a technical aspect to them derived from the common practices of bidding and contracting for construction work. But what has all this to do with literature?

To construct a graphic representation of the literary spectrum, we need to think beyond what we see in the project manual. If legal writing were pushed beyond contracts toward poetry, where would we be? And if technical writing were pushed beyond instruction manuals toward fiction, where would we be?

A simple diagram which illustrates the distinguishable types of writing from each other can be constructed as the accompanying drawing shows. And while each type has its own characteristics, rules, and

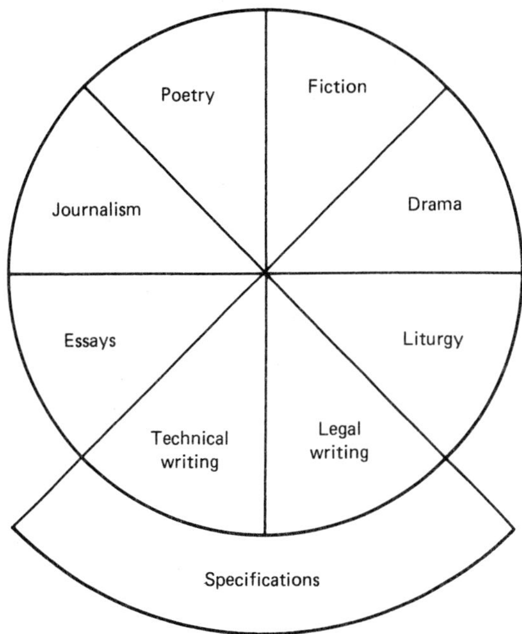

The spectrum of style.

classic examples, the lines dividing the segments are not always as clear and exact as they appear here. In practice, one kind of writing often merges into another. Plays sometimes verge on the liturgical, as in Aeschylus or T. S. Eliot. Fiction often becomes poetic, as in Faulkner or Joyce. Essays appear under the guise of journalism in newspapers and magazines. Specifications bridge the line between technical and legal writing in many ways. And we soon discover that literary style is a continuum as we move from one type of writing to another.

Here then is a map which shows specifications in the spectrum of style. Here too is an indication of where specifiers work as they scan countless drawings, read endless reams of manufacturers' literature, and tailor contract documents to the building projects at hand. Specifiers are not poets, nor were they meant to be, and yet with proper orientation they can continue to take a writer's pride in their craftsmanship while avoiding inappropriate excursions into areas best left to writers whose purpose lies elsewhere in the spectrum.

With a better understanding of themselves as writers among writers, specifiers may grow more sensitive to the use of language as a means of unambiguous expression while they purposefully strive to improve the clarity and conciseness of what they write.

chapter

13

Not by Specifications Alone

In trying to turn out a complete and perfect project manual, the specifier sometimes falls into thinking that if only everything is properly specified, then all will go well on the construction site. Unfortunately, experience indicates that even a perfect project manual does not guarantee a perfect job.

The contract documents, describing as they do a complex series of interrelated events, assemblages of hundreds of materials over a period of months or years by large numbers of workers and managers, can't possibly predict and resolve all the potential problems which may arise in the course of their execution.

The intent of the project manual may, in fact, be thwarted by any number of circumstances which are difficult or impossible to foresee: transportation or labor strikes; insolvency of subcontractors or suppliers; unanticipated subsurface conditions; unauthorized deviations from the contract documents; cost-cutting measures instituted during construction; and various other events which interfere with the regular progress of the work.

A good project manual is, therefore, not the complete answer to all the architect's problems; it's necessary but not sufficient. Clearly it's unreasonable to expect words alone to prevent all difficulties on the job during construction. For the most part, building problems that do arise are resolved as a part of the process of construction documentation, project administration, and field inspection, and in this process the project manual does play a central role.

Within the project manual, set forth in the general conditions and in project procedures, is a system of checks and reviews under which many participants examine each part of the work and pass on its accuracy, feasibility, completeness, and appropriateness. The system can accommodate changes, errors, and omissions from many sources and provides opportunities for correction in the normal course of the job.

At each stage of the work there are potential "checkers." During the documentation phase, the responsibility for finding problems is largely that of the architect and the architect's consultants. If a contractor or construction manager is on the team, he or she can begin to participate as well. For the specifier, the process begins with careful organization of the project manual, examination of drawings, and description of the materials and their installation. The first goal is to see that the drawings and specifications are as complete and accurate as possible.

The bidding period offers opportunities for contractors and subs to report any difficulties they find for correction by addendum, but the architect and consultants should still be examining their own work and correcting it. Cost estimators play a role at this stage, as do governmental agencies and owners who review the documents. Prebid conferences often reveal site or construction plant problems that may affect cost or execution.

Early in the construction phase, substitutions may be proposed as the contractor buys out the work. Evaluating substitutions and other submissions is critical to the success of the project and involves the architect's field inspection staff as well as the original specifier. The aim at this stage is to maintain the original character of the building and the integrity of the documents despite changes.

As the work proceeds into construction, the process continues through shop drawing review by the architect and consultants in which fabricators' details and amplifications of the contract drawings often result in additional corrections and changes. At the same time, inspection of the work in the field and, sometimes, of fabricated products in the shop may be required to see that the original intention is being carried out.

Throughout the progress of the work, many other activities contribute to the continuing examination of what is being done. Job meetings are important problem-resolving sessions at which architect, owner, contractors, subs, clerk of the works, suppliers, building inspectors, and others can deal with conflicts that have been discovered. Testing of materials, review of coordination drawings, and making of punch lists also help.

While the project manual is an important part of this system by which construction error is inhibited, the specifier should never forget that we build in an imperfect world where the vagaries of workers and supervision rule; where contending interests clash; where time, nature, and economics are not always on the owner's side. Recognizing the important role of the system of checks and controls, and the limitations of the project manual itself, is essential to specifying effectively.

chapter

14

Who Owns the Project Manual?

Architects and specifiers are generally familiar with Article 1.3 of the AIA General Conditions (A201), 13th edition, "Ownership and Use of Documents," which clearly states that "all Drawings, Specifications and copies thereof furnished by the Architect arc and shall remain his property," and that "they are to be used only with respect to this Project and are not to be used on any other project." Submission or necessary distribution of the documents in connection with the project "is not to be construed as publication in derogation of the Architect's common law copyright or other reserved rights."

Architects and specifiers are equally aware that, in reality, parts of their project manuals, including specifications, are frequently reused—reused by them on later projects, and reused by others who happen upon the documents. This practice is so common as to seem almost beneath notice until an aggrieved party decides to press the issue. Only then does one begin to ask how much of the specifications is original anyway? It's quite apparent that a specifier doesn't write each project manual entirely from scratch. A great many sections and parts of sections come from manufacturers' literature. CSI *Manu-Specs* are a ready source of material as well. Then, too, these days many architects use commercial masters such as *Spectext* or *Masterspec*. We are therefore dealing, at least in part, with material that in some form has probably been used a number of times already. If there is a copyright here, surely it belongs to the vendors and not to the architect.

As for the originality of the documents' organization, CSI's *Masterformat* (MP-2-1) and *Section Format* (MP-2-2) have made that largely uniform throughout the United States. To be sure, each specifier has an individual style and way of saying things, makes many decisions, and often expresses intent in carefully chosen language. But are such examples of style a suitable subject for formal copyright? After all, these are not literary works but the architect's instruments of service to a client. Would a lawyer copyright a will or a doctor an x-ray?

Reusing various pieces of the project manual is admittedly not the same as reusing the whole book. But because of the custom nature of architectural work, an entire project manual is seldom reusable without changes unless the new building is almost identical to the old, in which case accusations of plagiarism may have real merit. More often the copy at hand merely serves as a master for editing. Taking parts from several documents to fit the needs of a new project, far from being unqualifiedly reprehensible, really describes one of the basic activities of the specifier. The only question is, Where are the pieces obtained: from masters, from manufacturers, from standards-writing organizations, or from one's previous efforts or the efforts of others? Usually the answer is "all of the above."

What A201 really wants to prevent, however, is use of the drawings and specifications together to replicate at a new location a building designed by the architect for a particular client and site. Such unauthorized reuse would indeed damage the original architect and would most likely be actionable. Showing as they do the physical arrangement of materials and the dimensions critical to the building's appearance and function, the drawings, not the specifications, are the key documents in such reuse. To be sure, the contract documents are intended to be complementary, but specifications, while essential to a proper construction contract, can hardly ever be used by themselves to reproduce the designed building, which may be why architects have been loath to venture into litigation where specifications alone are involved.

Now just because reuse of specifications appears to be common and for the most part unprosecuted does not mean that this practice is without perils or problems for the inexperienced. The high degree of coordination, interrelationship of parts, and custom tailoring of a competent project manual to a particular building guarantee that there are more specifically applicable statements in a given document than might be expected. For example, each building has its own economic constraints and the copied specifications may indicate a higher (or lower) quality of materials than is appropriate for the new project. Too, different owners have their peculiar requirements that can only cause consternation (and expense) if misapplied elsewhere. And, once the original building's location is greatly changed, availability of certain materials through local distributors may be affected as may be use of other materials better suited to the previous conditions.

Under Article 1.3, architects clearly have rights in the project manuals produced under their stamps. But since the material is drawn from so many sources, some of them in (or nearly in) the public domain, and because without the drawings the project is so inadequately described, it behooves architects to proceed cautiously in prosecuting infringements.

chapter

15

The "As-Built" Project Manual

As part of the legacy of building turned over to the owner at the conclusion of construction, along with operating instructions and maintenance manuals, the contractor is often required to provide "as-built" or record drawings so that utilities can be located and further work facilitated at some later date. These drawings, prepared while construction is still in progress, with the parties who placed the work contributing their knowledge of what was actually done, generally prove invaluable in future years to maintenance staff, subsequent architects, insurance agents, contractors, and others who need detailed information about the building.

Drawings, however, only show shape, dimension, location, and relationship between components and materials (CSI *Manual of Practice,* MP-1-7) but don't identify products or methods of installation. Consequently, a great deal of information about what the building is actually made of resides in the specifications portion of the project manual. When the contract drawings are updated to as-built status, we have accurate information only on those things the drawings show. Years later, we often have little precise information (aside from what we can discover by examining visible and accessible portions of the building) about what products were used and how they were installed unless we also have the original project manual.

Yet even with a copy of the project manual in hand, we still don't have a reliable guide to what was built, for the demands of bidding and building fill a typical specifications section with a great variety of choices to be made during construction with the necessary decisions recorded in a collection of shop drawings, submittals, and correspondence that never find their way into the project manual at all. Thus, since specifications for many projects (especially those built with public funds) indicate several manufacturers for each product to encourage competition in bidding, or are performance specifications with no names included, it is usually difficult to find out later which of the specified options (or equal) was actually used. Worse, an unspecified substitution may have been accepted. Unaided memories of such events tend to be unreliable.

Of course, we can search through the shop drawings and manufacturer's data, if we still have the architect's job files. We can study the job records, correspondence, and change orders. We can examine operating and maintenance manuals if they have survived. But operating manuals won't identify those products that don't operate or need maintenance. And clearly, this is a tedious, time-consuming activity.

Since the contract edition of the project manual is such a questionable reference, how can we conveniently and consistently record what products were used on the job? One answer is to prepare an as-built project manual at the time record drawings are made. Assembling this equally useful product information in one accessible location is a logical way to end the construction phase and deserves an equal amount of effort and commitment from owner, architect, and contractor.

Lest this seem like an unmanageable quantity of work, even when done during construction, it should be said right away that not all of the project manual need be rewritten. Only the technical specifications require correction for this purpose, and only the Products portion (Part 2) of any section is really essential. If accurate notes are kept as products are approved, preparing an as-built manual should not be a difficult task.

Revising Part 2 of the sections will be even easier if the specifications are produced using automated data processing, since sections can be held electronically for later posting according to the job notes. Where the architect has the electronic originals he or she is in a better position to accomplish this, but it can be done manually and by the contractor just as well. Since this is not at present a routine service of the architect or contractor, it will have to be specifically required and included, like the record drawings, in the cost of the work.

Use of the as-built project manual may begin even during the guarantee period, as equipment is checked by the construction team. In addition, should the building be selected for publication in an architectural magazine, the product information likely to be required is at hand. It's equally useful as a reference in the architect's office to check on materials failure reports, so that future projects can benefit from the office's prior experience. In this way the as-built project manual can have an important role in improving the quality of professional services the architect offers to clients.

chapter

16

Plight of a Salesman

That endangered species, the manufacturer's architectural representative, has a difficult trade to ply. In order to satisfy their employers, manufacturer's representatives need to get their products specified on as many projects as possible. To do this they must make and maintain contacts in the architectural profession and in the building trades which furnish and install their products. Each manufacturer's representative tries to outshine the competition in an attempt to boost sales volume and meet company sales goals. Not only do representatives have to know what's being designed and where, but they may even have to take off quantities from the architect's drawings and price their materials for bidders. It's hard work that requires energy and optimism in large amounts.

Because one of the goals of manufacturers' representatives is to have their employers' products specified, they have to cultivate the interest of the architect and the specifier. To make themselves welcome in the office, representatives have to offer something that meets the architect's needs and fits into the process of producing the contract documents that constitutes the specifier's work and chief preoccupation. As a minimum, representatives must really know the product's technology, what it's made of, how it works, its applications, and its limitations. They are not going to get to first base otherwise. Representatives also need to know material and installation costs, since they will be asked often about these essential items. The value of manufacturers' representatives to the architect will be further increased if they can help detail the product in difficult or uncommon situations and if they are available for consulting and advising on product-related decisions. The specifier also wants representatives to warn about potential delivery delays or color and finish options which change or become unavailable. The best representatives visit the site during construction and verify that the materials are installed properly. In the end, representatives personify the manufacturer's guarantee: they can arrange for correction or replacement of defective materials to maintain the product's reputation. A manufacturer's representative has to do all of these things to merit the specifier's confidence and favor.

On the other hand, because one goal of representatives is to close sales and increase sales volume, they have to support the contractor or distributor who actually buys the material, who furnishes the cash, and who accepts the specification without substituting a similar material from another source. While the architect's primary interest may be the quality or design of the product, the contractor's primary concern is its eventual cost to the job. The representative may therefore have to sell the product twice (once to the specifier and once to the contractor) before having a real cash result. It's hard work indeed, but it can be done with intelligence, energy, and persistence. What happens, though, when the interests of the architect (design, quality) and the contractor (price, availability) come into conflict? Where does the representative stand then? How can he or she please both halves of the customer (and consequently the manufacturer) without alienating one side or the other? Sometimes it can't be done.

As a recent example, take the case of the area representative of a wood door manufacturer. For several years he had been visiting the office of a large architectural firm trying to convince the specifiers there to try the prefinished, premachined wood doors his company had been promoting. The specifiers were skeptical and asked lots of questions. It was hard to convince them that everything would go well with this technological innovation. Finally, the specifier agreed to use the new approach on a major high school building. Many hours were spent perfecting the language of the Wood Doors section, specifying the finish and coordinating this work with the Painting and Finish Hardware sections. The doors were a special size, over seven feet high, and of various widths. The finish was a dark stain on oak veneer. Some had matching transom panels. The job was bid and construction began.

Later in the year the representative appeared again at the office and asked to see the specifier. There was a problem, he said, and he needed help. Though the specification was clear, complete, and accurate, he had taken the order for the doors over the telephone from his distributor and passed it on to the factory without actually reading the specification. The doors had been finished at the mill in natural oak without the dark stain. Could the architect accept them anyway? The veneers were too thin to permit refinishing, the sizes were too odd to permit resale by recutting, and the distributor was too important a customer to be asked to absorb the loss if the doors were unacceptable. Unfortunately, all the other woodwork in the building had already been stained to match. A 180-door disaster.

What could go wrong, did. The salesman knew he alone was to blame, but that didn't help. Would those specifiers use his system again? Probably not. Would the manufacturer have to provide new doors and take the loss? Probably. Was anyone satisfied with this sale? No. And yet, it almost succeeded from every point of view: a large sale, the product of persistent sales effort; a model specification; and the acceptance of new technology. But whether in success or failure, the representative's role is clearly a critical one, and to balance this failure, many success stories can be told as well.

Though they may have a hard row to hoe, manufacturer's representatives do carry on a vital function in the construction process for buildings designed by architects. Not only do they keep the architect informed about new products and developments in the industry, but they act as needed go-betweens, carrying news and technology from field to plant to office and back. They are facilitators, easing the way to the use of products. And they are the visible presence of the manufacturer on the architectural and construction scene in the area they cover.

Though not heralded in specifications publications, or even very extensively in manufacturers' literature, the architectural representative is a truly important link in the construction chain. As manufacturers consider cutting their expenses even more severely during difficult periods, this important role needs to be preserved. Let's hope the representative's fate will be a lot better than that of the passenger pigeon and the heath hen.

chapter

17

The Unique Product and the Public Bidding Laws

Bidding laws and regulations which affect the construction of public buildings funded with tax dollars have a reasonable and honorable purpose: to assure that taxpayers get their money's worth. To obtain the best price for a given scope of work, all bidders must be placed on an equal footing and no preference can be shown one manufacturer to the disadvantage of others. Most such laws contain provisions permitting product substitution and call for at least three equal products to be specified in each case. As taxpayers, architects can generally endorse this purpose, though as architects they are acutely aware of the problems such a system presents.

While architects can accept legally prescribed

bidding procedures, rules for selection and substitution of products do not always appear consistent with their professional efforts to provide better buildings. In selecting products initially, architects often have trouble finding three or more identically functional, durable, well-designed items for each use, and yet they know that even others may turn up later when the often-mandatory phrase "or equal" is used in the specifications. A substitution proposed during the course of construction always threatens to mean something merely cheaper and less appropriate, perhaps by an unknown manufacturer or of greatly different character than originally envisaged. Though the architect is usually the ultimate judge of quality under the contract there is always an awareness that he or she acts under observation, potential criticism, and constraint.

Consider also the plight of the manufacturer's representative trying to promote a product in a competitive marketplace. The manufacturer's representative needs to convince the specifier that the product's unique features make it especially desirable. The representative's company may put great effort into developing new products and improving existing products. Discounts, credit arrangements, advertising, all stand behind the representative's drive to rise above competitors by providing something they can't duplicate, and yet government demands that each product be considered as merely equal to other similar items.

Though the architect may work to create a special building to satisfy the (public) client's needs, the building will be built, after all, largely out of common materials generally available to the construction industry. Even so, the materials will be organized and assembled to create a truly unique product—the building itself, an expression of the circumstances of its origin and of the designer's skill and vision. The added burden in doing public buildings is to develop and maintain the building's unique character without going beyond the limitations of product selection and approval imposed by the "or equal" philosophy.

Several specification techniques are available to help deal with this dilemma. All are discussed in the CSI *Manual of Practice*, MP-1-11,

"Methods of Specifying." Though naming three manufacturers and their products is the most direct response, the amount of research involved is considerable, particularly the first time around. Also applicable is the descriptive specification in which the product is only identified generically, with no manufacturer cited as a source. Of course, all important characteristics must be mentioned if no surprises are wanted when the proposed manufacturer's data are finally submitted. Performance specifications, another method, are often suggested as a cure-all, but are by far the most difficult and time-consuming to write since the desired results must be set down in great detail. Controlling the physical appearance of the product by this means is especially difficult, and the manufacturer's degree of latitude in approaching the problem is usually wide.

Other strategies exist for dealing with some of the more troublesome cases. Allowances can be established where artwork or some other undeniably unique product is required. Alternates may be permitted where new products or proprietary systems are desirable; but with alternates, the emphasis is still usually on low price, and unless the product is successful in the marketplace, it probably won't be selected.

The conflicts between uniformity and uniqueness, between special quality and low price are old ones and not easily resolved. The architect's challenge is to create public (and private) buildings which may be unique out of this variety of similar but not always equal products and processes. Many of the specifier's skills are needed to deal with the regulations of public agencies, particularly in the choice of products and the method of specifying.

It may well be, as a famous architect once said, that "God is in the details." Practical experience clearly indicates, however, that it's Caesar's project manual.

chapter

18

Alice's Restaurant

"You can get anything you want" at Alice's restaurant, according to the Arlo Guthrie song, and so it is with selecting products for buildings. The vast variety of materials available for construction is truly overwhelming until the architect's design intention, the client's special needs, and the specifier's experience are focused on choosing what is appropriate and setting it down in a preliminary or outline specification.

You can have anything you want, but deciding what you do want is where specifying begins. Though there are many products to choose and to choose from (an informal count identified some 2300 products in a typical elementary school), it is important also to consider just when is the right time to make materials decisions. Three stages of a project's development provide different opportunities and problems. Decisions made at a previous stage can be reinforced or reexamined later on, but always with caution.

The best time to decide on materials and products is during the first stage: when the contract documents are being developed in the architect's office, before they are printed and distributed to bidders. Then there is time to do research and explore options. Manufacturers' representatives are available, and literature not on hand can be sent for. All affected parties can be consulted and products coordinated for consistency of design and function. If the owner or a funding agency requires three products to be specified for each use, this is the time to undertake the necessary investigation to see that they are reasonably equal and that their appearance is acceptable.

In spite of a job well done initially, questions thought previously settled are frequently revived during the second stage, the bidding period. Salespersons whose products were not mentioned begin calling to have their materials added by addendum. Even if study eventually reveals the merits of such products, it's not wise to add them formally at this time since the door is then opened to a host of additional similar requests. Considerable time and energy can be spent in researching a variety of products which in the end may not be carried by the successful bidder. If you have already named three products, that's generally enough to base bids on.

During the construction period (the third stage), requests for substitutions can really begin to pile up as shop drawings and manufacturers' data arrive. What is a good policy for handling this inevitability? Flexibility is surely required, but also firmness. A reasonable position is to specify carefully during the first stage, naming acceptable equal products, and then to insist on getting what was specified. Even so, consideration of other products is sometimes justifiable. In any case, it should be remembered that the architect is the judge of whether a proposed product is equal to the one specified. The architect is just as responsible for failure of an approved substituted material as would be the case if it had been specified originally. Herein lies the need to examine substitutions carefully and to try to reduce the always-present pressure to decide quickly and accept hastily in order not to hold up work at the site.

To investigate an unfamiliar material or product properly, the architect needs time to assemble data and samples, to verify performance by consulting other reputable users, to order tests when essential, and to examine the proposed material and its method of installation thoroughly. When the number of proposed substitutions is large, the time commitment becomes a matter of great concern. It's far more economical to have done the analysis during the document preparation stage.

Often the substitution request is motivated by a cost advantage to the contractor, not necessarily in the owner's interest. A standard letter may prove useful in such cases: "Before we investigate this product, we need to know what credit the owner will receive if it is approved." A quick cost-benefit calculation can then be made before proceeding. This may be countered by the contractor's standard ploy, "Yes, we can get what you specified, but it will delay the job" (often because it wasn't ordered in time, but that's not mentioned). Tough decisions have to be made under such pressure, but decisions on materials which affect the building's safety, weather-resistance, or function shouldn't be made hastily or casually.

As the architect, you must choose the appropriate products for the buildings you design. Part of choosing wisely and getting what you want lies in making decisions at the right time in the project's sequence. Even Alice closes the restaurant sometimes.

chapter

19

Games Contractors Play

Since specifications are the technical portion of the agreement between the owner and the contractor, it's important for the specifier to know how to prescribe most effectively exactly what the contractor is to do in the course of constructing the building. In instructing the contractor and subs about how certain parts of their work are to be done, the specifier needs to know not only what options are available but also what mistakes are likely to be made. It is necessary to ask how the work might be done in an unacceptable way in order to prevent that from happening by giving specific instructions and by forbidding certain detrimental actions.

Because twenty or more trades and hundreds of activities are often involved, the goal of preventing anything at all from going wrong by writing the specifications carefully is hard to achieve in practice. There is always likely to be something left unmentioned, something overlooked or unanticipated, or something left to the contractor's decision. This uncharted area can be quickly turned into a source of conflict if the contractor is so inclined.

Even where the documents are excellent and the instructions clear, things can still go wrong on the job. Specifiers are often heavily involved in resolving construction phase problems not of their own making but which call upon their technical background and knowledge of the construction game in its entirety.

Although many contractors are capable and intend to do the work as bid or negotiated, there are some who seem to find their own interest diverging from that of other members of the building team at times. While the specifier's main opportunity to deal with such divergence is in the preparation of the project manual itself, the game isn't over when the bids are received; on the contrary, it is often just beginning.

Here are a few of the games contractors sometimes play. There are many others and variations are constantly being invented.

Substitutions

A favorite pastime. You have listed six acceptable paint manufacturers. The contractor submits a seventh (an unknown). Should you call out the chemistry research lab? You are offered an unfamiliar roofing or waterproofing membrane "just as good" as the one(s) specified. Do you search for evidence from ten prior satisfied users? The burden of proof is on the contractor in such cases to convince the architect that the proposed product meets the job requirements. Provided the specifications were carefully thought out and well-drafted initially, this game can be played at the contractor's expense, not the owner's. But be satisfied you are not giving away the store before accepting the substitution.

Highball

"Galvanizing the steel lintels will triple the price and take 10 weeks. We didn't bid it that way because nobody galvanizes lintels anyway." This is a test of the architect's willingness to stand behind the specifications. A phone call to a galvanizer or two might bring the price and the timing down to proper scale. But the specifier needs to have a good idea of the cost and availability of what he or she specifies to deal with this game.

Credit Card

If you left something out and have to add it, you always pay more; if you deduct something you did include, you never get full credit. True, there are administrative costs in both cases which the contractor is due in all fairness. But sometimes the numbers get out of hand and we are off into playland very quickly on either the up or down side. Limiting unit prices by providing for add-only sums and deducting a uniform percentage for decreases (say 10 percent) helps bring some control to this popular on-site game.

Mail Order

"Yes, we can provide what you specified, but it will delay the job (because we didn't order it early enough), so please accept our (cheaper) substitution so we can get the project done on time. Otherwise the delay will be your fault." Should there have been a critical path diagram for this job which included lead time for this item? (Or maybe it was too small to warrant attention at first.) This game needs stopping in the shop drawing and data submission stage. It may be hard to do now.

Special Delivery

"I know it's not exactly what you specified but they just delivered it to the site and I don't want to send it back (delay, expense) so can't we please unload the truck right now? It's four o'clock and the workers go home in half an hour." How did we get into a spot like this? Didn't we get shop drawings and manufacturers' data approved before shipment? How did it get this far before anyone checked? Will we have to take an unwanted credit for defective work not remedied?

The project manual is still the rule book for playing the building game, but rules are sometimes subject to interpretation; and if someone cheats, a friendly game may turn sour. With large amounts of money at stake, the temptation to play games is often compelling. A certain amount of worldly wise understanding of the construction process is useful to the specifier and experience in the field on construction sites is unquestionably valuable.

It's important to remember also that it is by compromise, adjustment, and alternate solutions that problems get resolved on the site, and that the specifier can have a key role in playing (and winning) the games that are played there.

chapter

20

Games Owners Play

The previous chapter dealt with the owner's and the architect's specifications problems resulting from contractors' actions during construction. But there are often significant specifications problems between architect and owner as well, and these should receive equal attention.

It's true that the architect is the owner's agent for the project, but he or she also has a responsibility to the public for whose health and safety the architect is licensed, and to the work, on which the architect's professional reputation depends. Thus the architect cannot always be the owner's "yes-man" but must maintain an independent position if his or her professional and technical advice is to have value.

Each party to the contract has a role, and the

owner's is not to write the project manual or to dictate its contents, though the owner does need to make informed decisions about what is to be done. Many problems stem from an owner's well-intentioned but unwise attempts to direct the architect to do things experience and training warn against doing. Here are a few games owners sometimes play.

I'm In Charge

Thinking that a percentage of the architect's fee can thereby be saved, the owner decides to hire the consulting engineers without making them responsible to the architect. The owner intends to coordinate the work in a "hands-on" way. It seldom happens. The task of coordinating a construction project's many parts is so inextricably bound up with what the architect does, that the architect's having little contractual control over consultants almost always results in omissions, confusion, gray areas of responsibility, duplication of effort, and far less coordination than a project (especially a large one) really needs.

The specifier is in the middle of the coordination effort at the documentation stage, and generally has great difficulty under this arrangement in coordinating the specifications effectively. The usual result is that the project manual is incomplete or conflicting and many construction phase problems are engendered. Aside from trying to establish cooperation with such consultants on a personal or professional basis, there is little the specifier can do to pull the different disciplines together. The small portion of the fee "saved" by this game is generally spent quickly during construction when the contractor sits down at the table to play.

Expert

If the owner thinks the architect is weak in some area important to the project, a specialist may be hired to deal with the problem. Often the specialist has sold the owner on the need for such services, but however the specialist enters the picture, the question raised is the same: Who has the responsibility? If the expert makes suggestions, is the architect obliged to accept them? If the expert writes a specification section, who is responsible for the results? What is the specifier to do when the expert's specification affects other trades adversely? If an expert is really needed, it's usually far better for the architect to retain him or her and thus to preserve the authority that is needed to carry out professional responsibilities.

My Rules

When preparing a project manual, most architects use AIA General Conditions because they are familiar, have stood the test of litigation, and have generally been accepted by legal and contractor groups, signifying some degree of consensus. But what if the owner has other ideas? "We don't use AIA conditions in this state" or "That's what I have lawyers for" are sometimes heard. And, while contractors can always make their objections to contract conditions effective by refusing to bid the project, what can the architect and specifier do when they are obliged to use general conditions in which the architect's role is poorly stated or inhibited during the construction period, or conditions in which traditional procedures for conduct of the work are so changed that confusion and hazard may result?

While most public authorities have standard conditions that roughly parallel AIA documents in content, if not in organization, and are generally acceptable with reasonable modifications, what the private owner's lawyers can devise varies widely. In such cases the architect is well-advised to have his or her own attorney review owner-supplied general conditions to be sure that the architect's role and responsibilities embodied in them are consistent with the owner-architect agreement the architect has signed and with the architect's professional obligations under law.

The specifier has the additional problem of determining the effect of such conditions on other parts of the contract documents and of seeing that the conditions themselves are consistent with good practice and the resolution of practical problems that may arise during construction.

A special case occurs when the owner hands over general conditions from a previous project for reuse. The specifier must then check to see that the type of contract is the same (construction manager? lump-sum? separate prime contractors?) and that the new location, building type, and owner-architect agreement are all consistent with what has been done under dissimilar circumstances somewhere else.

Guess What?

Many things that are going to be discovered during construction are difficult to know in advance. Subsurface conditions are only indicated generally by test borings and surprises are always possible. In remodeling and renovation, once parts of existing buildings are demolished, unforeseen conditions often appear. Utility maps are sometimes in error and records of previous work can be inaccurate. It's always best to allow for such unknowns in the contract documents by using unit prices, assumed quantities, allowances, and other techniques that have been developed for just this purpose over many years of construction experience.

If the owner, through lack of sophistication or anticontractor bias, demands that the contractor be responsible for the costs of unanticipated conditions, the owner is generally asking for an expensive advantage. To be sure, the owner may want a firm price for the construction, and an upset maximum price can be given, but it's not usually the lowest price available since the contractor can't accurately price unknowns. If the owner can carry a contingency amount and live with some uncertainty, a better deal can usually be struck. If the owner wants the contractor to guess about conditions, the contractor will also have to guess the cost of meeting them in a lump-sum bid. Where the contractor alone bears the uncertainty and the cost of being wrong, the owner shouldn't expect the price to be low.

Rush When I'm Ready

"Time is money" is as true of construction as it is of other activities, and in construction the numbers are generally big ones. The owner is always in a hurry to begin building and continually presses the architect to shorten the time needed for document preparation. But owners often seem totally unaware of the time they take out of the production schedule by delaying decisions they must make and by prolonging review of documents and conditions. Rarely is the owner prepared to proceed at the same speed demanded of the architect. True, some architects have trouble deciding too, but waiting for the owner's untimely decisions can frustrate and delay even the team which is ready and able to proceed with its work. Laying out the decisions to be made often helps the owner choose among options. But the specifier sometimes has no choice except to set aside those sections dependent on the owner's unmade decisions, even though the original completion date will have to be met regardless of the owner's dilatory behavior. An alternative approach is to specify by default, saying, "If we don't get a decision, this is what we'll do." It's usually better to have specified something, even if it has to be changed later, than to leave everything for the very end when the answers are finally available but time has run out.

Muscle

From time to time the specifier will receive an owner's direct order to use a certain product without option and without permitting substitutions. Sometimes the owner has a financial or other interest in the product or manufacturer and an outright "no" would be tactless on the specifier's part to say the least. It *is* the owner's money, of course, and he is entitled to spend it any (foolish) way he wants to. But if the product is inferior, inappropriate, or otherwise unacceptable for the particular building, what can be done? The answer depends more on the degree of seriousness of the problems raised by use of the product than it does on questions of principle alone.

In any case, the specifier will have to research the characteristics, limitations, and track record of the product to be sure he or she is on firm ground before taking a position. If the adverse effects of such use would be minor (shorter useful life, increased maintenance, less elegant appearance), the specifier is probably better off yielding on the issue to avoid friction in the owner-architect relationship. If the product is likely to present some real hazard to public health or safety, the architect will have to oppose its use (preferably in writing) giving reasons and urging reconsideration. Failure to convince the owner leaves little recourse but to place responsibility on the owner for results (also in writing), but this will not generally be accepted graciously. The most difficult case occurs if the product doesn't fall neatly in either of the above categories or if the results are unpredictable or uncertain. Better to resist, but how much and how intensely? How many times can the architect and specifier confront the owner to preserve their professional judgment and reputation while still preserving a good relationship with their client?

A case of Muscle occurred on a recent publicly funded project when the specifier received a telephone call from a staff member of the state authority which was the client. "Use Joe's windows on the job," he was ordered. The specifier properly replied, "I'll be glad to as soon as I receive this instruction in writing with your signature and some technical information about Joe's windows. I've never used them before." No written order was ever sent.

Wholesale

The owner may be in a position to purchase a product (like carpeting) cheaply as a large-volume buyer or may already have on-hand materials or equipment to be used in the new building. There's nothing wrong with specifying that the contractor is to install under the contract material furnished by the owner, and most contractors have little objection to doing so. But unless the owner furnishes detailed information about such products, it may be difficult for the specifier to describe their proper installation and for the contractor to price the work. Unless the material is new and of standard or familiar character, the specifier should inspect it before writing about it. Neither the specifier nor the contractor should be made responsible for installation of inappropriate, damaged, or inadequate materials that the owner has somehow obtained.

chapter

21

Stanford Revisited

When CSI commissioned the Stanford Research Institute to study current practices in the use of automated techniques for specifications some 15 years ago, few firms had gone beyond automatic typewriters and punched paper tape. Charles Diehl, the study's prescient author, identified six levels of possible automation, the first four comprising the existing state of the art. Level I, manual preparation of project manuals, was not included in the study.

The majority of firms surveyed used automatic typewriters for level II work, which Diehl called "automatic typing or printing," or for level III efforts, described as "specification storage, retrieval, and modification using automation." A few used computers (largely IBM 1130s) for level II or III tasks. A few were using computers at level IV, "advanced techniques for storage, retrieval, and modification of specifications." Large computer systems were also available for them and for the even fewer in the vanguard of level V, "future integrated design and specification production systems using computers." Level VI was reserved for unidentified future systems.

The Stanford study (now unfortunately out of print) was important for the profession not only because it outlined what was then possible and what was being done at the time to automate specification production, and not only because it inspired creation of the Construction Sciences Research Foundation by CSI, but more important, because it was the first systematic analysis of the process so many architects and specifiers engage in when they produce project manuals (by whatever method). Diehl perceptively characterized specifications as a medium of communication among the many sectors of the construction industry (see Appendix A) and he identified the principal users of the project manual in a many-armed "spider" diagram (see the accompanying illustration) that clarified and confirmed the central role specifications have to play.

The study (properly) concentrated on the potential gains in productivity that automation offered and directed attention to the changing role of the specifier under the new circumstances: at level III (the takeoff point), the specifier becomes predominantly concerned with preparing master documents for the system. At level IV and beyond, the specifier is a technical consultant and resource person. The intervening years have seen several service groups arise to help the specifier provide and maintain master specifications as more firms arrived at level III. And recognition of the specifier's decision-making role has increased correspondingly as level IV systems became feasible.

During the same period, equipment grew more sophisticated, with many specifiers working through remote terminals connected to large mainframe time-sharing systems. The increasing capability of word processing equipment has encouraged larger numbers of architects to do their project manuals on the smaller office-size units now in use across the country. Still, what is remarkable after such a short time is not the increasing variety of hardware available, but that so few regular

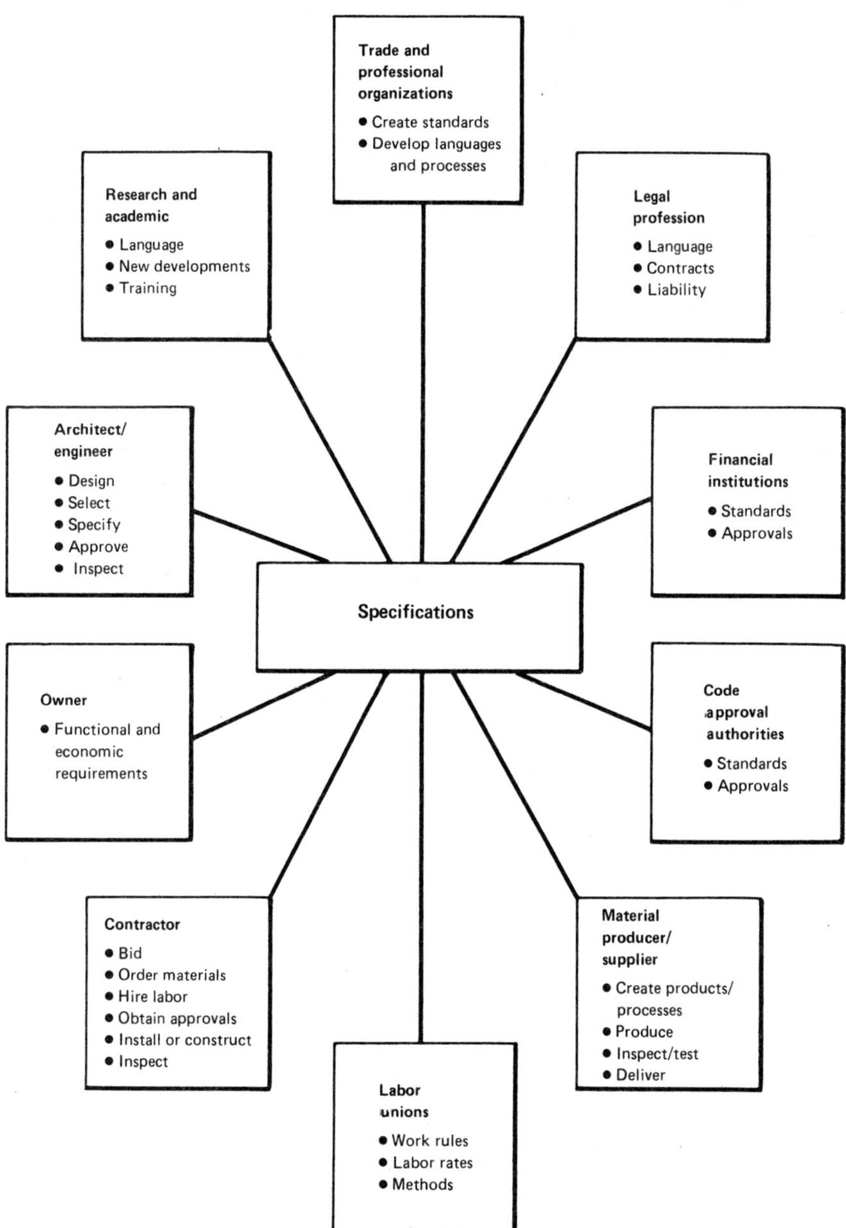

Principal participants in the specifications communications process. (From Charles V. Diehl: "Automated Specifications, A Research Survey," STD-1. Alexandria, Va.: The Construction Specifications Institute, November, 1967, p. 18.)

producers of project manuals are today using less than level III methods.

While the report revealed that architects interviewed at the time had not yet begun to employ computer graphics, Diehl was aware of experimental integrated systems being developed in university settings. As architects become more experienced in computer-aided design and drafting, the once vanguard level V seems to be gaining reality. Diehl may not have foreseen the rapid development and deployment of powerful smaller systems, but he did understand the general direction that automation of the architect's work would take.

There is much of value still to be learned from the Stanford Research study even though the state of the art has moved well beyond its 1967 description. The basic perception and analysis of the needs of specifiers and the process of automated specifications still ring true. Today's emphasis on automating the design and drawing portions of architectural work does not mean that specifications have declined in importance or centrality. Nor will the specifier's role as consultant and technical adviser soon diminish. Clearly, the knowledge of applied building technology will always be essential to both design and construction, regardless of the form documents produced by the architect may take.

Perhaps it's now time for a new independent study of advanced techniques of document production. In addition to revealing the character and extent of the many changes that have already taken place, such a study would show where we currently are on the road to an integrated system of design and documentation. Until this is undertaken, however, the Stanford report, despite its technological obsolescence, will probably remain the best exposition we have of what producing specifications is all about.

part 3

The Specifier's Role

chapter

22

The Compleat Specifier

If one were to specify the ideal person to hire or to work with in producing a project manual, what would he or she be like? Would this specifier resemble anyone you know or work with now? In addition to generally desirable human and professional virtues, what are the special qualities that characterize the ideal specifier? Is this idle speculation? Perhaps. But it's potentially helpful nevertheless in discovering, interviewing, and training candidates for this role in the architect's office.

Part 1. General Characteristics

1.01. Technical Curiosity. Possesses more than a normal amount of technical curiosity. Wants to know the names of things, materials, skills, and trades. Wants to know what things are made of and how they are put together. Wants to know how things work, how they are done, and under what circumstances.

1.02. **Observant.** Is a very observant person, alert to what is seen in books, on building sites, and everywhere else. Has a good memory for the above as well as for details of drawings, buildings, and manufacturers' literature.

1.03. **Fact Finder.** Is a fact finder investigating the processes going on all around: in the office and on the site, in the fabricator's shop, in the industrial plant, and in the brickyard. Is a natural researcher who soon figures out where to go for information: what books, what people, what records, and what tests can be relied on. If what has been seen or what's behind it all is not fully understood, this person takes action to find out. Continually adds to his or her storehouse of information and knowledge and keeps it current.

1.04. **Economic Concern.** Is concerned that things be done economically, both in his or her own work preparing project manuals and in the contractor's work on the building which is being described. Takes the view that the right way is the best way and eventually the most economical way.

1.05. **Legal Concern.** Has a feeling for the unambiguous phrase and the legal implications of the specifier's activities when writing contracts for construction, dealing with the interests of different parties, and the rules of law and of government.

Part 2. Materials and Skills

2.01. **Architectural Work.** Is familiar with the profession of architecture and how architects work. Has spent several years drafting, detailing buildings, and preparing working drawings. Understands project management in the office and project administration during construction.

2.02. **Writing.** Has good verbal ability. Thinks logically and analyzes situations and circumstances accurately. Reads quickly and effectively gathers information. Writes clearly and directly using as few words as are needed for completeness. Is particularly good at clarifying confused expressions and in editing the writing of others.

2.03. **People Skills.** Understands how people work, including contractors, architects, and owners. Understands how they do their jobs and how they relate to each other. Is knowledgeable about the organization of the construction industry and uses this knowledge in dealing with problems.

2.04. **Technology.** Is an expert in building technology. Knows the work of each trade and how each task should be done. Knows how buildings go together in the field, the sequence of events, the jurisdiction of trades, and the constraints that affect what is or is not done. Knows how and where each material should and should not be used. Knows the relative cost of various materials, products, and ways of building.

Part 3. Application

3.01. **Organization.** Is a good organizer, able to orchestrate the efforts of many contributors to a project for the purpose of producing the project manual. Is looking for shortcuts in the interests of efficiency, not sloth. Is inventive, even creative at times.

3.02. **Systems.** Is systematic and consistent in setting up and carrying out work. Looks for regularity, uniformity, and consistency in the work done. Is flexible but not careless. Is thorough but not trivial. Is persistent but not disagreeable.

3.03. **Strategy.** Is like a chess player, developing a strategy, carrying out moves in accordance with a planned design, always trying to anticipate the next move of the architect, the owner, contractors, and workers at the site. Wants the answers to questions about what to do or who is to do it to have been provided and detailed in the contract documents. Wants the solution to problems to be foreseen in the project manual before the actual occurrence. Seeks to play the perfect game.

3.04. **Production.** Plans and controls the production of the project manual and anticipates time required so that deadlines are met. Uses word processing and data processing equipment to reduce repetition and improve speed and accuracy. Understands what goes on the drawings and what belongs in the project manual and is not easily confused by those who don't.

3.05. **Style.** Applies skills and knowledge in a way that is thoughtful, realistic, practical, perceptive, and sympathetic to the design goals of the office.

Not every specifier has or could have all these characteristics in the right balance and amount, of course; but the closer to the ideal one gets, the better specifier a person is likely to be and the happier and more successful in this work. If you discover such a person in the making, offer encouragement and help to develop these valuable skills. If such a person works for you or with you, value his or her abilities and contributions. If you need and are looking for such a person, may your search be rewarded by finding the ideal specifier. And if you aim to be such a person, let's hope your situation provides the work opportunities, the training, the experience, the encouragement, and the rewards you will surely deserve should you succeed.

chapter

23

Evaluating New Products

The relatively new field of energy-related products and equipment, particularly for active solar heating systems, has once again brought into focus the architect's role in evaluating new materials for buildings. Traditional procedures of examining the product itself, the manufacturer's data, the theory under which the product was designed, and the recommended installation procedure, are all essential steps and valuable in predicting the product's potential for success. But while building is to some extent a science, it is a very practical science and depends on experience to validate its practices. Thus the ultimate test of a new product is its durability and usefulness in the field over a period of time, and it is precisely these characteristics that are so difficult to determine in advance.

The product itself gives clues to its future when examined under the specifier's experienced eye.

Early solar collectors often used multimetal connections (steel casings with copper connectors, for example) which invited galvanic activity in exposed locations and which could be safely predicted to have substantial corrosion problems within a short time. In later models, plastic fittings separated the metals. The specifier who examined the early model carefully didn't buy it as offered; but the right questions had to be asked. Eventually, the National Bureau of Standards (and others) began developing performance and testing criteria for solar collectors to aid in system evaluations.

Manufacturers subject their materials to accelerated use and weather tests (as well as other tests) to convince specifiers and themselves that their products will perform well and will endure. But laboratory conditions (even outdoors) are only simulated-use situations, and the way in which the product is actually handled and installed may be quite different. Yes, we need these tests, but we also need to know how to interpret and understand them. Early literature on inverted roof systems seemed to indicate a well-thought-out theory of roofing which responded to the causes of many roof failures. The theory seemed sound, but would it work on the roof? Only time and many successful installations gave a satisfactory answer.

The results of actual use in a variety of applications and conditions are the ultimate evidence we seek, but it can't be had easily on new products. Who is willing to try a new product outside the laboratory so that we can get the information needed to specify with confidence? If we divide building into arbitrary categories, one answer suggests itself. Surely the architect and owner are hesitant to experiment on an institutional building where long life and low maintenance are important. Only tried and proven materials would seem to be appropriate for this use. But there is a sector of the industry which is willing to take risks in return for financial rewards, and if the new product can save money, it will find a receptive audience there. Even small unit savings when multiplied by large quantities are attractive; and as long as the risks are clearly delineated and accepted by the owner, this might well be one entry point into the system for a new product, energy-saving or otherwise. How long the product needs to be in use before it can be confidently specified depends, therefore, at least partly on the acceptable risk factor for the segment of the building industry in which the architect is working.

Of the three types of documentation, laboratory data (on which the manufacturer relies), product data (on which the architect relies), and field feedback (on which the architect, manufacturer, and owner rely), the last is the most difficult to obtain quickly, and often the most difficult to obtain at all. Thus the specifier, who must examine all three, plus the product itself, needs a degree of cautious optimism (or pessimism, depending on his or her experience) in approaching new products until a substantial amount of evidence is in hand and the product can finally be accepted or rejected for a particular use.

This is not the total process by which products succeed or fail in the architectural marketplace, but it is a part of it. New products developed to meet energy conservation needs, particularly those which form part of the exterior fabric of the building (rather than those components of mechanical systems which are close developments of existing similar equipment), also need to pass the time-in-use test before they can be routinely specified on a variety of major building types. Not such exhilarating news for manufacturers perhaps, but consistent with the cautious eighteenth-century admonition which litigation-shy specifiers might well consider adopting: "Be not the first by whom the new is tried nor yet the last to lay the old aside." Some old-fashioned advice to modern specifiers from the English poet Alexander Pope.

chapter

24

Comprehensive Specifications Services

Writing down descriptions and installation requirements for materials to be used in the work; preparing precise instructions to bidders and special conditions under which the project will be bid and built; organizing, collecting, and coordinating all the written documents to form the project manual—these are specifiers' ordinary services, basic to their traditional role in the profession.

To perform such services competently, specifiers must know construction practices, materials and methods; as well as the availability, relative cost, and proper use of each material and its limitations. They need to know the organization of construction, the interrelation of the different parts of the work, and the roles of the various participants in the building process. They must also understand how buildings are represented in working drawings, how drawings are translated into buildings in the field, and, importantly, the effect of materials choices and methods of construction on the architectural character of a building.

In addition to eliciting information from the project manager, team members, and consultants, the specifier spends a lot of time studying progress drawings for information about what is to be built and how it will be put together. Since each material indicated must also be specified, a search to identify every item and its use is essential to preparation of technical specification sections. Often the specifier has previously been a drafter or a project manager, but now views the drawings with a more analytical eye, construction-conscious and trade-oriented. In fact, the specifier's view is rather close to that of a contractor preparing a bid, except for the latter's concern with quantities.

Looking at the drawings from this somewhat different viewpoint, the specifier is more likely to see inconsistencies, potential construction difficulties, inappropriate use of materials, and similar problems which might otherwise escape notice until later when the contractor examines the finished set. Out of this combination of technical knowledge, documentation experience, and construction perspective, usually channeled exclusively into project manual production, arises the potential for significant additional service to the architectural team. The specifier's ability to offer early review of design or working drawings and to help in identifying and resolving materials and construction problems can take him or her far beyond the specifier's traditional role with great resulting benefit to the project.

It should be remembered also that the full-time specifier has probably been through many more projects than the typical job captain of equal years and may therefore have a better overview of the structure of contract documents for a building. As a result, the specifier is in a good position to suggest directions with regard to bidding strategy, choice and extent of allowances and alternates, timing of bidding, and length of bid period when these are being discussed. The specifier is well able to set up the bid form and advise on the advantages of lump-sum versus cost-plus-fee contracts to obtain optimum results for the owner in a particular case. And the specifier is generally the best-qualified person to judge what assignment of work to different trades will afford the greatest construction economy.

The extent to which these additional services are offered and used on a project depends to some extent on the relationship between the specifier and team members, particularly the team leader. What appears threatening or intrusive will surely be resisted, so that the specifier's "boardside manner" will either help or hinder the process. Where the specifier is in-house, a full member of the project team, it should be easy to take advantage of this potential help. But enough time must be allowed so that the specifier is not overwhelmed with competing deadlines and conflicting commitments. Under pressure to finish the project manual quickly, the first casualty is usually the time to discuss details and to help work out solutions to construction problems. On the other hand, if the specifier is a consultant, his or her time is paid for in a fee, which may not be sufficient to allow any but the most narrow interpretation of responsibilities. Even when time permits, the consultant may not offer comment or constructive criticism unless the architect requests it and provides an atmosphere (as well as a contract) that encourages it.

Little evidence of the inherent capacity to furnish more comprehensive services is apparent in common job descriptions for specifiers, nor is the subject discussed directly in CSI literature to any significant extent. Yet experienced project managers know how valuable it can be and experienced specifiers find this aspect of their work the most challenging and often the most rewarding, confirming as it does the centrality of their role in the process of construction documentation.

chapter

25

Being There

One of the best ways for the specifier to get valuable first-hand information about what's going on in the construction world, about the relationship between what is specified and what is built, about the conditions and circumstances under which buildings are put together, is to visit a construction site on which specifications he or she has written are being used. If out of convenience, economy, or mere laziness, someone else is sent, the results just won't be the same, either for the office or for the specifier. For when the architect goes on site, his or her attention is on design and coordination matters and the need to deal primarily with the building's contractors, subcontractors, and the client. Even if there is time, the architect is not as intensely familiar with the products being installed by many trades as is the specifier, and it is only the exceptional architect who even notices whether the sealant being applied is a polyurethane or a polysulfide.

The precise product name, number, manufacturer, and approved method of installation are the meat and potatoes of the specifier's workday life. Trips to the site make more real the catalog cuts and descriptions which the specifier deals with daily in a way that samples and data never can. But because there is often a considerable lag period between the writing of the project manual and construction sufficiently advanced to make a trip worthwhile, it is important to review the contract documents before setting out on the tour. To avoid excessive memory clutter, most specifiers tend to debrief themselves after completing each project manual in order to make room for the next job in their minds where many conditions and products are continually being scanned and sorted as work on the contract documents for the new project progresses. The refresher is therefore usually needed.

Upon arriving at the site, it's easy for the specifier to recognize familiar materials already installed. The constant question in mind is, Are these the materials that were specified? What is also noticed is the method of installation, accompanied by a mental check as to whether the application is the one specified or approved. A third series of observations concerns the conditions under which the work is being done, for this too is an important part of the project manual's scope. Of course it's simple-minded to imagine some superspecifier performing this building inspection in any systematic or thorough manner, going through all sixteen divisions trade by trade, and it's not likely to happen. Too many products and processes are involved. But among the many things done right, some that don't appear right will catch the observant specifier's eye, and benefit to the proper construction of the building and to the specifier's store of knowledge may result.

Useful detailed information about things gone wrong on the job all too rarely makes it back to the specifier unless it's something really serious, expensive to correct, or particularly embarrassing to the architect. Not because no one cares, and not because it wouldn't be helpful (clearly it would), is this feedback so hard to collect. It's usually because there are too many things to do, too many urgent problems to be solved in the field, and because once solved, such matters are easily forgotten. Thus the occasional visit to the site is all the more valuable for the specifier trying to improve the quality of the documents he or she produces.

Information that hardly ever gets back to the specifier in the office includes, for example, the weather conditions under which products were installed; how and where materials were stored on the site before being used; or what techniques were being employed for laying concrete block or mixing waterproofing. Just by observing the empty cartons and scraps of materials on the ground or in the dumpster, the specifier learns more about what was incorporated in the work that day than any clerk-of-the-works would ever report.

Being thoroughly familiar with the general conditions of the construction contract and the usual organization of projects by contractors, the specifier should know enough not to mention his or her observations and not to comment on what is seen to workers on the site. The proverbial bull in a china shop might be considered a delicate, graceful figure compared to a representative of the architect who marches around the building pointing out errors and calling for changes to anyone within earshot. Clearly this is not the mission. Whatever contributions the specifier has to make to improving the conduct of the work or more properly carrying out the contract requirements are obviously better held for the architect's review and the specifier's future information. Yes, there is a responsibility to report serious mistakes and errors, but it needs to be done through the architect to the contractor's superintendent and not in random fashion.

So far the visit described has been during some middle stage of construction, but there is value also in the specifier's trip to the site around the time of substantial completion as well. Only then can most of the finishes and completed sections of work be seen. The specifier can even participate in the preparation of the inevitable punch list of items to be corrected before final acceptance. If the building is substantially complete and partly occupied, observations about early wear and failure in use will be made for future reference. A tour of the building toward the end of the one-year guarantee period is also useful, as further indications of products performing well or failing after this time can lead eventually to a list of "don'ts" for the specifier formulating office policy on such materials for future projects.

Just as no young Victorian considered an education complete without a tour of Europe, no modern specifier can operate knowledgeably solely from the shelter of a remote office. There's just no substitute for being there.

chapter

26

Games Specifiers Play

While it has been observed that contractors, architects, and owners occasionally behave somewhat deviously in common project-related situations, it may be less frequently admitted that specifiers too have been known to indulge in game playing in order to overcome obstacles presented by others in the course of their work. It's not that the direct approach doesn't work; it usually does. Yet there are times when special weapons and tactics are required to carry out the coordination, documentation, and execution of the project in spite of such obstacles. Here then are a few games specifiers sometimes play.

Shell Game

Three manufacturers are required for each product by a government authority's zealous enforcer. That's okay for most products (the office master has three of each already researched anyway), but what about the occasional product only made by one or two manufacturers? What to do? Under some jurisdictions, it's acceptable to list the available two and for the third to state "No other known manufacturer." If that doesn't satisfy requirements, perhaps an existing not-quite-right third product will work with some modifications. Or the specifier can always write (at length) a descriptive or performance specification for the item. Just inventing names isn't a good idea. Naming two versions of the same product by different suppliers doesn't usually work either. When the contractor goes out to buy one of the shady versions, the specifier will be found out, and, if the product is imaginary, the embarrassment will be real.

Guess What?

Domestic and overseas owners, wanting maximum product competition (or fearing collusion between the architect and manufacturers or suppliers) sometimes give instructions not to use any manufacturers' names in the project manual, but just to describe the products desired. It's time-consuming and tedious, but the specifier can do this if it's really necessary by using national standards (ANSI, ASTM, AWPA, DIN, BS, etc.) and carefully indicating all characteristics of the product.

The trouble arises when the documents are out to bid and the contractors start calling. "What is this thing, who makes it, and where do I get it?" they'll ask. Since the "descriptive specification" is usually based on some real-world product (otherwise it can't be bought) the specifier knows its name and model number, and (owner permitting) can give out the information verbally even though he or she is forbidden to write it into the project manual. In these cases it's prudent to keep a loose-leaf scrapbook near the phone arranged by *Masterformat* or specification section index with cuts and manufacturers' data on all the products to help answer the bidders' questions when they call. On occasion the owner may even ask for a copy when reviewing the specifications before bidding. The field staff will also need a copy during construction in order to check on contractors' submissions. This is not the specifier's game of choice, since it is so indirect and time-consuming, but he or she can play it well if necessary.

Trade-off

If either of two trades can do it, which one should be chosen to do it by including the work in one trade's section or the other's? For example, interior brick paving (depending on thickness) can be set by masons or by tile setters. The degree of precision wanted, the type and thickness of jointing, and the cost of labor are factors to be considered in making the choice. Should certain sash be shop-glazed or field-glazed? Again, cost and work sequence determine which section gets the write-up. Should plumbers or drain layers do piping lines on site outside the building? Labor cost, type of pipe, and type of joint will determine which way to go. Where the work is specified generally determines how it will be assigned and bid. To play this game the specifier needs to be aware of trade jurisdictions, trade practices in the locality, and even area wage rates. It's best to investigate thoroughly before deciding where to specify such items.

Left Overs

Take access panels. It's hard to predict exactly how many will be needed on some projects. Aside from carrying a unit price (complicated by the product's variety of sizes and installation situations) what can the specifier do to be sure all the necessary panels are included in a lump-sum bid? Since most panels are required for access to mechanical equipment, it's logical to assign responsibility for furnishing them to the mechanical sections. A special panel for dumbwaiter machine access, for example, can be covered in the Dumbwaiter section. But what about other access situations that are difficult to predict exactly?

The buck stops with the general contractor when the specifier requires, under Miscellaneous Specialties or a similar section, that "All required access panels not furnished under another section be furnished under this section" with typical panel sizes and situations described for pricing. All the bases are now covered and the panel counting is done by the contractors pricing the work (who are responsible for quantities anyway) rather than by the architect.

Is this a sly game? Not really. As long as the responsibility is clearly assigned and pricing is possible, the specifier's task has been adequately performed. And, what is just as important, no gaps in the work are left since all panels are provided in one section or, by default, in another. Without this strategy there is often a moment during construction when representatives of the general contractor and several subcontractors are all standing around the field office disclaiming any responsibility for access panels at all since they were not included in each one's section of the project manual and no one carried them. The result of this scene is usually that the owner is faced with an annoying (and often expensive) extra to the architect's embarrassment.

Not Yet

In dealing with an indecisive or inexperienced designer or project architect, it's often difficult to complete specifications which depend on decisions being made in useful sequence. There are only so many sections that can be completed before needed but unmade decisions can bring things to a halt. One tactic of desperation generally applied at the last minute is for the specifier to make the decision and tell the architect: "This is what I have specified. If you want something else, I'll gladly change it, but until you decide what should be used, this is what you are going to get on the project." The advantage of this approach, in addition to clarifying the decision that needs to be made, is that it allows completion of the documents and pricing by contractors without further delay. The disadvantage—unless the specifier is a sophisticated player—is that what is finally decided upon may be more expensive, require greater lead time to obtain, or entail changes or modifications to other sections of the specifications at an inopportune later moment. Of course it's best to get the right decision at the right time. Playing this game is the specifier's second-best solution.

Insurance

The manufacturer has a new product which seems suitable for the project, but it hasn't been used very often (or ever before) in the United States. It looks okay, but what if it doesn't do the job? Of course there are manufacturers' guarantees (limited, of course) and implied warranties, but how do they help the owner who is depending on a system that fails to operate? In some cases the specifier can set forth alternative actions the manufacturer (or contractor) must take if the equipment doesn't perform. Or the specifier can require cash payments (not damages) so that the owner can hire alternative means of doing the job until the equipment functions as it's supposed to do.

An innovative hospital drug- and record-conveying system was specified in this way to protect the hospital from costs it would incur if the system failed to operate as designed. The hourly cost of hiring orderlies to carry the materials to their destinations in the building complex was included in the contract. In case the system downtime exceeded twelve hours, the contractor's payments would support an alternate way of getting the items distributed, since the owner could not go longer without the service after occupancy nor should the hospital have had to pay for manual delivery after substantial completion of the building. Fortunately the system operated as planned, and the indemnification was never needed. However, since it was spelled out, each party's risk was evaluated and agreed on. This game is useful when success is reasonably certain but a hedge against failure is needed.

Such special tactics as these are developed by specifiers after similar repeated incidents in order to overcome the inevitable frustration which would result if no remedy were sought. Making life easier for the specifier just sometimes makes doing the project manual and the project a little easier as well.

chapter

27

Specifier's Holiday

The master specification is up-to-date. All the bids are in. Everything else is in preliminary design. What's a specifier to do? There's always literature to read or research to pursue, but how can a specifier earn money for the architectural practice when there are no project manuals to be done for a while? Here are a few suggestions.

Since specification writing itself is a marketable skill, the specifier can start by seeking other clients to write for. The architect's consultants (acoustical, equipment, or landscape, for example) may need help in preparing written documents for their clients on other projects. Or, architects in other firms might welcome an experienced specifier's aid in meeting their short schedules. Building owners, especially institutions, often need specifications done for their own in-house work. Even manufacturers preparing model documents for architects to use are potential clients for the available specifier's talents.

A second area for fee-producing effort is the review of specifications prepared by other writers. Here the clients are institutions, agencies, building owners, and other architects. The review can be for completeness and consistency, to discover any errors, or to check the quality of materials specified and the methods of application for appropriateness to the building type and budget. Evaluation of proposed bidding procedures for best strategy and compliance with public bidding regulations are additional useful services that take advantage of the specifier's special familiarity with the legal aspects of project manuals.

Moving into the field, the specifier is usually well qualified to visit completed buildings on behalf of owners, architects, agencies, or manufacturers to examine the in-place performance of building materials and assemblies. If failures are discovered, the specifier is usually able to recommend corrective measures, or at least indicate the direction of further investigations. The specifier's hard-earned knowledge of what materials are appropriate for each use and how they should be installed is basic to this type of investigation, which often leads to reports and recommendations to the client as to future policy on the use of questioned or failed materials.

If a connection with a manufacturer can be established, either directly or through an architectural representative, the specifier can offer his or her services to review proposed or published product literature from the "buyer's" point of view. The specifier's critical study of the sales approach and presentation, as well as the completeness of essential information, offers the manufacturer valuable feedback and useful knowledge about how the product is being received.

Beyond reviewing literature and inspecting products in use, the specifier with extensive experience can offer to evaluate materials proposed for use in large quantities by owners, agencies, institutions, or even manufacturers. Although not generally a laboratory technician, the specifier knows how to evaluate test data, make investigations of users' experiences with such products, and report results with recommendations to concerned clients.

If none of the above approaches prove fruitful, the specifier is still well-prepared to talk to technical groups and to teach about materials and methods of construction in technical schools and adult education courses. Many specifiers have served as guest faculty in architectural schools across the country, earning fees, but at the same time broadening their contacts and familiarizing others not only with their subject matter but also with themselves and the practices they represent. A related activity that produces modest income is the writing of technical and semitechnical articles for trade, industry, and professional magazines whose readers have an active interest in subjects the specifier knows well.

These general groups of income-producing activities use the many construction-related skills specifiers have acquired in the normal course of their work. Few of them can be activated instantly without advance preparation and client development. All return dividends well beyond the actual fees earned in public awareness of the specifier's role and the contribution made by the specifier to the successful practice of architecture. This may in fact be the most valuable reward the specifier receives from such efforts, even though the architect will certainly appreciate the additional money.

And if all else fails, there is still one more way in which most specifiers can help their architectural practices: putting in a few weeks on the drawing boards not only produces an obvious economic benefit but can also help keep the specifier in touch with the other side of the profession—the graphic part on which the specifier's usual work continues to depend.

chapter

28

Specifier's Nightmare

If specifiers have awakened in the middle of the night during the past several years, it may be the nightmare of obsolescence which invaded their dreams and raised fears about their continued role and even their future existence as part of the construction team.

There is a degree of realism to these fears, which stems from the automation of specifications production starting in the late 1960s. In a system of totally automated contract document production, is there a place for the specifier?

"The traditional role of the specifier starts to change in Level III (automated) systems; he becomes the writer of the master specification rather than a producer of individual job specifications" according to CSI's Stanford Research study.

And at higher levels of automation, with integrated computer-aided design and drafting (CADD) systems turning out contract drawings as a by-product of architect's decisions that are recorded electronically, together with specifications furnished by software suppliers to supplement digitized takeoffs and unit prices in the system, where is there room for the specifier to contribute to the project?

Even before software suppliers take over, a multitude of master specifications producers have already entered the field: government agencies, CSI, AIA, and other private vendors are all offering (annotated) specifications in hard-copy form and in a variety of electronic forms as well.

Manu-Specs by manufacturers, *Spectext*, *Comspec*, office masters, and further automation, while taking time and tedium out of the process, have also tended to narrow, or at least to redefine to some degree, the specifier's role. To many alert observers, the user-friendly master specification often appears to be replacing use of the friendly specifier, and hence the cold sweat in the small hours of the night.

In large offices, traditionally the bastion of the dedicated specifier, advances in automation have been accepted early, and the standardization of procedures and policies, which is the forerunner of automation, has been the most rapid and the most profitable in this setting. A result of this evolution has been to make specifying more easily done well by the nonspecialized architect or engineer.

Who then will write the project manual in the future? Is it the project architect? If the architect does all the design and production drawings on computer-aided graphic equipment, no doubt he or she will also edit the specifications on the same equipment. And if the drafter completes a detail drawing on the machine, he or she can also be responsible for the specifications that go with it. Under this regimen, the specifier is merely a custodian of the master in the system or the modifier of the specifications software to match the details the architect wants to use. Even so, there may still be a need for someone in the office to pull together all the specifications work of the people who produce such a project by automated means, to add the appropriate contractual conditions and bidding information, and to see that it all fits together properly. It's specifier's work now, but the project architect may be the one left to do it in the more fully automated future.

If the project is a standard building type which is produced over and over again using the same materials and products with only variations in dimensions and layout, one specification package will probably do it anyway, except for special site conditions which may need to be dealt with. Specifications in this case are a one-time effort and there is little continuing role for the specifier. But where custom, unique, or special buildings are being documented, the specifier may still be needed, automation or none.

Where anticipating construction phase problems is important and where materials decisions have to be made during design, the specifier will still be a useful resource. Where new materials are involved which require investigation and evaluation before use, the specifier will still be needed to carry the process through the stage between manufacturers' literature and actual acceptance of the product for the particular project.

Where bidding strategy, cost control, and product history are factors, the specifier will continue to be a valuable asset. Where substitutions and alternates require evaluation during and prior to construction, the specifier's experience and judgment will still be of use.

Where the architect needs help relating the products and materials to be used to the character and design of the building, the specifier's knowledge and experience will still be valuable. And where coordinating the specifications work of consultants (who may or may not be a part of the architect's CADD system) needs to be done, the specifier's skills will still prove to be the right ones for the job.

For, just as it is today, a great part of the construction industry of the future will still be producing custom buildings. It will still be sensitive to site, economics, and technology. There will still be a great variety of owner interests, governmental regulations, institutional procedures, and many different contractual arrangements which greatly affect building. There will always be differences of approach, design, and detailing among architects. (Just consider, for example, how many types of corner treatment for concrete columns are used today.) Buildings will still have different characters and personalities, as will the architects and owners who produce them, and although these differences may be handled by automated methods in the architect's office, in the end someone has to oversee and maintain the quality of what goes into the machines and what comes out of them.

Unless many other things change as well, the architect will continue to have final responsibility for that quality. Whether the architect does it alone or relies on others, including the specifier, will depend on the size of the project, the degree of specialization and automation in the office, and the time available to do the many tasks involved in putting a project together. Either the architect or the architect's associates will take on the specifier's role (as often happens today), or a specially trained person will have the assignment; but the things that need doing will still require the kind of experience and judgment described here.

Maybe the specifier's role will be more diffused; maybe it will be easier; maybe there will be fewer specifiers who don't do anything else. Maybe we can't honestly say "There'll always be a specifier." Maybe we can't, but for the foreseeable future it's still a good bet.

part 4

Appendixes

appendix

Specifications—A Medium of Communication

Specifications, in the simplest description possible, serve as one of the two basic media of communication in the construction process, and, in most instances, are accompanied by drawings to form the construction documents. The drawings are primarily visual expressions of the geometry of the item to be constructed, with the specifications providing verbal descriptions of its quality, color or pattern, and performance characteristics. This point will seem trite to the construction fraternity, however, it is made to stress that *we are, in essence, talking about automation of a communication process*. (Italics added). This process is one in which the sender, or initiator of the message, is informing others of an action, process, or material that is to be incorporated in the construction of an item through a *written* medium.

Charles V. Diehl: "Automated Specifications—A Research Survey," STD-1. Alexandria, Va.: The Construction Specifications Institute, November, 1967, pp. 16–20. Reproduced with permission.

If the message is garbled, or has a lot of static, its meaning may be lost to the receiver, and the communication process has failed to varying degrees. Because this failure could result in economic loss or physical injury, the basic aim is to produce a communication which is, to the extent economically practical, error free.

Techniques of automation lend themselves to the capability of reducing error, particularly in repetitive processes. Properly designed automation processes often provide supplementary economic benefits, and relieve the human mind of repetitious and often boring tasks. The pursuit of automation for automation's sake is seldom justified except in research and development processes. The pursuit of practical automation in the specification process does not fall into this category. The court calendars provide evidence that the communication purpose of the specifications is not always successful; therefore, any basic improvement in the process has tangible and real benefits.

The Senders and Receivers of the Specification Message

Figure 1 [See p. 103 of this book.] is a representation of the principal participants and their actions in the specification "communication." This figure provides some measure of the complexity of the specification communication process. Although the message may be transmitted in the same form to each of the receivers, the purpose for which the message is used by these receivers is not the same. The problem in writing specifications is to write one message that can be received and understood by many receivers, each of whom may take a different action as a result of receiving the same message. To partially overcome this problem of multiple interpretation, the sender often reserves the right to approve the actions initiated by the message. Approval of shop drawings, materials, equipment, and site work may complete the process initiated by the specification. The specification message is, therefore, not a "send only" type of message, but results in many feedback messages. The result which hopefully will be obtained through this multiple exchange of communications is an item constructed to the intent of its owner.

Because there are no real industrial giants (designer-producer-contractor) involved in the total construction processes, the communications that have been developed to date are not sophisticated. The fragmentation of the construction process goes even further because of the sheer number of owners, designers, contractors, and material suppliers who are involved. Construction is one of the remaining fields which falls in the category of a large "cottage industry." Although no one who appreciates good architecture or engineering would suggest that every building should be built from the same design, there is no reason not to employ the same basic systems in achieving many phases of the construction process. It is felt that the industry can standardize the construction processes and systems without standardizing the end product.

The argument that every item of construction is different does not *per se* make it valid to say that it is not feasible to automate or standardize the systems that program, design, and construct buildings or other works. The sheer numbers of different organizations involved in the process provide a sound basis for standardizing the communication process to the maximum extent possible. Multiple receivers must be able to receive the specification message in an ungarbled fashion. The techniques and equipment available today make it possible to overcome many of the past communication deficiencies that have existed in the construction process. For the industry to close its eyes to these opportunities for improvement in an area that absorbs much of our national and private dollar is, at least, short-sighted. To those who are reluctant to make the effort to improve the process, it may represent personal or organizational disaster. Robert Wehrli, University of Utah Architecture Department, stated recently,

> Computer-aided architectural services are now as inevitable as sunrise tomorrow. The question is not if architects will be practicing by computer, but only when and by whom. Perhaps this is a question of boon or doom for the profession and especially for the small office.[1]

These observations may not seem germane to a survey of automation techniques for specifications. The old story of the man who asked two construction laborers "What are you doing?" may help to clarify the point intended. In response, one replied, "I am shoveling dirt"; the second responded, "I am building a cathedral." The specifier, in like vein, is not just writing, but rather communicating in the construction process, and is a part

[1]The Computer—Its Current Role in Architectural Education, Association of Collegiate Schools of Architecture, Washington, D.C., 1967, p. 28.

of a whole chain of communications. To be successful in his role in the process it is not only necessary that his communication be clear, but that it can be effectively used by all concerned in the process. Although there are substantial benefits to be obtained from the use of existing automation techniques, the current state-of-the-art can only be considered as being in its embryonic stages in general practice. Few firms have been involved in significant automation for over three years. More substantial benefit will accrue when the system of recording construction data, then re-recording the same data for the next step in the process, can be improved to eliminate the number of times in which data must be translated by laborious manual processes. Technology has provided most of the means to improve the process, but the general environment of the construction industry is not amenable to change because of the tremendous fragmentation that exists in all of the elemental processes involved. One of the significant problems is not just how to automate, but how to provide the environment so that automation can be done successfully at a reasonable cost.

In addition to the fragmentation within the construction industry, the buyers of the industry's services are also fragmented. This again poses additional problems. Even the large government construction agencies vary internally from office to office in the type of language that is to be provided in the construction documents; large industrial firms likewise have specific firm policies. As a result, the larger A & E firms find that they have as many as six different master specifications to maintain. In some instances it is only the General Conditions that vary, but in many cases even the basic requirements for structural steel and concrete specifications are changed. This inability to reach common agreement results in each job being more or less tailor-made. The time spent in tailoring items that could be standard from job to job results in economic waste. Although the client may not be paying for this effort directly under the fee system, indirectly he is losing the time that could be spent in the more creative processes to produce a better facility. The time spent on specification writing job by job could be better used to perfect master specifications and improve clarity, or in materials research.

Contract documents are legal documents. As a result the legal profession has much to say about their content. The stress from many of the firms interviewed was that the liability of architects and engineers for the adequacy of their work was being more severely felt over time. During a recent discussion, Professor H. Wheeler, Pennsylvania State University, indicated that liability for design is becoming an important factor in the design professions (based on a study he recently completed). This again points up the need to use specification language which has passed the test of actual use and application, to the greatest extent possible. The rewriting of specifications for each job may provide a challenge to the writer. It also provides an opportunity for his writing to be tested in legal proceedings in or out of court. The need to improve and clarify the language of specifications on a systematic basis is becoming just as important as the need to maintain current references on new materials. Automation of the specification system provides the opportunity for technical as well as economic improvement.

appendix B

Add-Only Unit Prices

An example (from a bid form) of the unit price system in which only "add" prices are given for extra work, with provision for ten percent reduction in unit prices for decreased work. This method is used to insure more accurate pricing by contractors. See Chapter 19.

UNIT PRICES: Should certain additional work be required, or should the quantities of certain classes of work be increased or decreased from those on which the General Bid is to be based, by order or approval of the Architect, the undersigned agrees that the following supplemental Unit Prices will be the basis of payment to him or credit to the Owner for such addition, increase or decrease in work. Unit Prices given shall represent the exact net amount per unit to be paid the Contractor (in the case of additions or increases) or to be refunded the Owner (in the case of decreases). No additional adjustment will be allowed for overhead, profit, insurance, compensation insurance or other direct or indirect expenses of Contractor or Subcontractors. Refer to Sections listed in parentheses below for description and measurement of Unit Price items. The Owner shall have the right to reject any or all proposed Unit Prices at any time prior to signing the Agreement, in which case the cost of extra work shall be as determined by one of the other methods set forth in Article 12 of the General Conditions. Unit Prices given herein shall be for additional work only. Decreased work at Unit Prices shall be at the "Add" price less ten percent (10%).

SCHEDULE OF UNIT PRICES	ADD
1. General site excavation by machine, removed from the site, per cubic yard. (Section 02200).	$________
2. Trench excavation by machine, removed from the site, per cubic yard. (Section 02221).	$________
3. Additional ordinary fill, compacted, in place, per cubic yard. (Section 02221).	$________
4. Substructure concrete in place, including forms, reinforcing and stripping, per cubic yard. (Section 03300).	$________
5. Exterior caulking, including joint backing, 3/8" wide, per linear foot. (Section 07900).	$________

appendix

Outline Specification

This appendix provides a sample outline specification showing a variety of abbreviated sections to accompany early drawings at the design development phase. This outline specification is provided for illustration purposes only and should not be used on any project without thorough professional review.

Examples of proprietary, descriptive, and one-line requirements are included. Some sections are more fully developed. This type of outline can also serve as a checklist. A more elaborate and complete outline specification would result from following the method described in Chapter 1.

OUTLINE SPECIFICATION

PROJECT NAME
CITY, STATE

THE ARCHITECT'S NAME
STREET ADDRESS
CITY, STATE 00000
TELEPHONE NUMBER

PROJECT NO.

DATE

INDEX

DIVISION 1: GENERAL CONDITIONS
DIVISION 2: SITE WORK
DIVISION 3: CONCRETE
DIVISION 4: MASONRY
DIVISION 5: METALS
DIVISION 6: WOOD AND PLASTICS
DIVISION 7: THERMAL AND MOISTURE PROTECTION
DIVISION 8: DOORS AND WINDOWS
DIVISION 9: FINISHES
DIVISION 10: SPECIALTIES
DIVISION 11: EQUIPMENT
DIVISION 12: FURNISHINGS
DIVISION 13: SPECIAL CONSTRUCTION
DIVISION 14: CONVEYING SYSTEMS
DIVISION 15: MECHANICAL
DIVISION 16: ELECTRICAL

PROJECT IDENTIFICATION

Section 00700: General Conditions

A. General Conditions: Use AIA Document A-201, 13th Edition August 1976.

B. Supplementary General Conditions: Use Architect's Standard.

Section 02000: Excavation and Site Work

A. Protect all existing, active utility lines. Plug, cap or remove all existing inactive utility lines.

B. Clear and grub site as indicated and specified including legal off-site disposal of all debris.

C. Demolition to grade will be done under another Contract.

D. Legally dispose of all excavated materials off the site which are unsuitable for fill.

E. Establish permanent benchmarks. Replace monuments and other reference points which are destroyed or disturbed.

F. Excavate, trench, and backfill as required for footings, foundations, walls, slabs, paving, utility lines, mechanical work, catch basins, manholes, and other below-grade work indicated on Drawings, specified or required. Provide necessary shoring and bracing of excavations to protect work and assure safety. Maintain excavations free of water.

G. Excavate rock as required.

H. Provide ordinary fill, structural fill, and backfill. If sufficient suitable fill is not available from excavation under the Contract, additional fill shall be brought to the site at no additional cost to the Owner.

I. Provide drainage fill for use under interior slabs-on-grade and at footing drains.

OUTLINE SPECIFICATIONS Page 1 of

PROJECT IDENTIFICATION

J. Do all rough grading and spreading, compaction, and control of fill to conform to lines and grades indicated on the Drawings and details.
K. Provide drain lines.
L. Construct manholes and drain inlets where required.
M. Protect and retain existing building foundations.
N. Remove existing pavement.

Section 02440: Site Improvements

A. Provide bituminous drives, walks, and parking areas and paint parking lines.
B. Construct concrete retaining walls, steps, and walks.
C. Do all brick paving at plazas.
D. Provide concrete curbs.
E. Provide granite curbs and sloped granite edging.
F. Provide exposed aggregate concrete paving and flagstone courtyard surfaces.
G. Furnish and spread topsoil. Plant and maintain lawns.
H. Plant, fertilize, and maintain ground cover, trees, and shrubs as indicated on Drawings.
I. Provide lawn irrigation system connected to water lines, drainable and frostproof.

Section 03000: Concrete

A. Furnish all necessary labor, materials, equipment, and appliances to construct all precast and poured-in-place concrete work.

OUTLINE SPECIFICATIONS Page 2 of

PROJECT IDENTIFICATION

B. Provide plain and reinforced concrete footings, foundation walls, slabs-on-grade, stairs, platforms, underground conduit casings, and all other concrete incidental to a complete job.

C. Install polyethylene film vapor barrier under all interior slabs-on-grade. Provide premolded expansion material at expansion joints. Provide rigid perimeter insulation.

D. Forms for concrete shall be smooth plywood. Concrete shall use ASTM C-90 Type II cement for concealed work and Type I with selected aggregates for exposed work.

E. Reinforce slabs-on-grade with wire mesh. Bar reinforcing shall be intermediate grade, new billet steel conforming to ASTM A-615 for deformed bars.

F. Exposed Concrete Finish: Form-tie cone depressions shall be retained and filled to within 1/2″ of surface. Control joints shall be formed with wood strips. Construct two (2) sample concrete panels 4′-0″ × 2′-0″ × 4″ thick for approval of forming and finishing techniques.

G. Precast architectural concrete shall be made with Type I or Type III cement and selected aggregates. Include attachment devices to structural steel. Sample panels will be required.

Section 04000: Masonry

A. Concrete block shall be non-load-bearing ordinary cement and gravel or crushed stone units with load-bearing units meeting ASTM C-90 and C-145 as applicable.

B. Pumice block shall be lightweight textured block meeting ASTM C-90. Block shall be of uniform color and shall remain unpainted in the finished work.

C. Profile block shall meet physical requirements of ASTM C-90

OUTLINE SPECIFICATIONS Page 3 of

PROJECT IDENTIFICATION

and ASTM C-216 Grade SW for facing brick. Compressive strength shall be not less than 3000 psi. Color shall be as selected from samples.

D. Face brick and pavers shall be New England water-struck solid clay brick without cores conforming to ASTM C-216, Grade SW, Type FBS.

E. Install all anchors, bolts, ties, fastenings. Place lintels and built-in flashing as required.

F. Vertical control joints shall be located not more than 25 feet apart and as shown on Drawings. Horizontal reinforcing shall be 9-gauge galvanized steel placed every other horizontal joint.

G. Jointing shall be concave tooled.

Section 05000: Miscellaneous Metal Work

A. Fabricate and install all pipe and tubular handrails, brackets and inserts, steel ladders, access panels, and aluminum louvers other than unit ventilator grilles.

B. Build steel stairs, including pan treads and landings to receive concrete fill.

C. Provide aluminum thresholds, expansion joint covers, and abrasive stair nosings.

D. Furnish all metal inserts, dovetail slots, anchors, fastenings, etc., for attachment of work of all trades to concrete or masonry and all lintels.

E. Provide extruded aluminum mat frames.

F. Provide site ironwork, including manhole covers and frames

OUTLINE SPECIFICATIONS Page 4 of

PROJECT IDENTIFICATION

and catch basin inlets of heavy-duty gray iron castings. Access ladders in manholes shall be asphalt-coated wrought iron rungs.

G. Provide miscellaneous metal for elevators.

Section 05100: Structural Steel

A. Structural steel shall generally be ASTM A-36 steel. Use A-242 steel where indicated.

B. Shop connections shall be welded. Field connections shall be high-tensile bolted using "turn-of-nut" method.

C. Provide mill reports for steel.

D. Connections shall develop full strength of members.

E. Clean all steel in accordance with SSPC procedures.

F. Steel exposed in finished work shall have No. 6 blast cleaning.

G. Prime with approved shop coat.

H. Erect all steel furnished under this Section. Provide all required temporary guying and bracing until final connections are complete.

Section 06000: Carpentry and Millwork

A. Provide all general carpentry including that required by other trades.

B. Provide all rough framing, centers, blocking, grounds, furring, nailing strips, etc.

C. Furnish and install all rough hardware, bolts, nuts and washers for carpentry work.

OUTLINE SPECIFICATIONS Page 5 of

PROJECT IDENTIFICATION

D. Provide all interior wood finish.
E. Install finish hardware.
F. Provide treated wood nailers for roofing.

Section 06400: Cabinetwork

A. Furnish and install all wood casework and cabinetwork.
B. Work shall conform to AWI Custom Grade Standards for Materials and Workmanship.
C. All cabinets shall be shop-finished.
D. Include shelf standards, pulls, hinges, locks, and all other cabinet hardware.

Section 07000: Waterproofing and Dampproofing

A. Provide cold trowel application of asphaltic mastic over all exterior foundation walls of habitable and storage rooms below grade from bottom of footing to 4 inches below finish grade.
B. Include fiberboard protection for mastic.
C. Do all mastic coating of steel embedded in masonry.
D. Provide interior membrane waterproofing under ceramic tile beds at toilet rooms.
E. Furnish fabric flashing for building into exterior masonry.
F. Provide fluid-applied liquid membrane waterproofing at horizontal deck surfaces, two-part asphalt-modified polyurethane system.

OUTLINE SPECIFICATIONS Page 6 of

PROJECT IDENTIFICATION

Section 07250: Sprayed-on Fireproofing

A. Use mineral fiber type without asbestos.

B. Thickness shall be as required to meet required ratings.

Section 07500: Roofing and Sheet Metal

A. Built-up roofing all roof areas shall be 40# base sheet and three plies of 15# felt, 20-year bond, gravel surface.

B. Base Flashing: Built-up asphalt and felt, 20-year endorsement.

C. Cap flashing and all other flashing required shall be 16-ounce copper, lead-coated where exposed to view. Furnish and install sheet metal reglets and expansion joint covers.

D. Pipes through roof shall be flashed with 16-ounce copper.

E. Roof insulation shall be equal to 2″ rigid fiberglass board and vapor barrier mopped in two layers.

F. Furnish and install roof hatches, unit sky domes, and smoke vents.

Section 07900: Caulking

A. Exterior Caulking: Caulk all doors, window frames, louver frames, masonry-to-concrete joints and other openings. Include caulking setting bed for door saddles.

B. Interior Caulking: Caulk all masonry-to-concrete joints, window and door frames, mop receptor joints.

C. Exterior Caulking: In general, use two-part polyurethane.

D. Use one-part acrylic sealant at perimeter of exterior door and window frames.

OUTLINE SPECIFICATIONS Page 7 of

PROJECT IDENTIFICATION

E. Interior caulking shall be oleoresinous.

F. Use joint backer and joint primer recommended by sealant manufacturer.

Section 08100: Metal Doors and Frames

A. All interior metal door frames and glazed partitions shall be 16-gauge pressed steel, exterior frames, 14-gauge.

B. Exterior metal doors and interior fire doors shall be hollow metal with 16-gauge steel faces, glazed as shown. Provide UL labels where required by code.

C. All other steel doors shall have 18-gauge faces.

D. Provide metal transoms and louvers for metal doors where required.

Section 08120: Aluminum Entrance Doors and Frames

A. Finish shall be bronze-anodized aluminum on KE-45 or 6063 alloy.

B. Use dry glazing method. Weatherstrip doors.

C. Use tempered glass in doors and sidelights.

D. Include all hardware for doors except lock cylinders.

Section 08210: Wood Doors

A. Wood doors shall be solid staved core flush face doors 1¾″ thick, AWI Custom Grade.

B. Cores shall be AWI Type A; face veneers shall be AWI Type 1.

OUTLINE SPECIFICATIONS Page 8 of

PROJECT IDENTIFICATION

C. For paint finish, use rotary-cut birch. For natural finish, use plain-sliced red oak. Edges shall be of matching hardwood.

Section 08510: Steel Windows

A. Steel window frames shall be fixed and heavy intermediate weather-stripped casement type, with frame and vent weighing approximately 3.5 pounds per foot. Frames shall have baked shop finish coat.

B. All operating hardware shall be extra-heavy-duty-type polished bronze. Opening sash shall be provided with polished bronze operators and two cam fasteners per sash.

Section 08520: Aluminum Windows

A. Provide aluminum frames and windows to meet NAAMM Standards for C-A2 construction.

B. Finish of all aluminum shall be anodized Duranodic Bronze, AA-M12-C22-A42 on KE45 or 6063 alloy.

C. Casements shall have welded ventilator corners, bronze roto operators, and bronze cam fasteners.

Section 08700: Finish Hardware

A. Hardware will be furnished under an Allowance.

B. Provide three (3) butts per door, ball-bearing butts on high-use doors. Include closers.

C. Panic hardware as required, shall be concealed type.

OUTLINE SPECIFICATIONS Page 9 of

PROJECT IDENTIFICATION

D. Masterkey locksets to Owner's key system. Locksets shall be mortise type.

E. Toilet room doors shall have push plates, pulls, and closers.

F. Provide lock cylinders for aluminum entrance doors.

G. Finish of all hardware shall be dull chrome (US26D) or stainless steel (US28).

Section 08800: Glass and Glazing

A. Glass for exterior windows shall be "Solar Bronze" as manufactured by Pittsburgh Plate Glass Company, Libbey-Owens-Ford, or equal.

B. Insulating Glass: shall be 1" thick units with ½" air space. Outside light shall be Solar Bronze. Inside light shall be clear.

C. Interior glass shall be ¼" polished plate or float glass.

D. Exterior glazing compound shall be acrylic or silicone type meeting Federal Specification TT-P-791-A. Glazing beads shall be metal throughout. Provide glazing tape, setting blocks, spacer shims, etc.

E. Do interior glazing in standard glazing compound.

F. Provide square mesh ¼" plate wire glass, Pittsburgh "Baroque" or equal where required.

G. Provide mirrors over each toilet room sink, ¼" polished plate silvered back with painted sheet metal backing and chrome-plated brass channel edges.

Section 09200: Lathing and Plastering

A. Provide all lathing materials and accessories including steel stud and track system, gypsum lath, expanded metal lath, channel furring, and suspension system for ceilings.

OUTLINE SPECIFICATIONS Page 10 of

PROJECT IDENTIFICATION

B. Do all plastering. Use gypsum plaster at all interior surfaces. Use cement plaster stucco at exterior walls and soffits. Provide scratch coat for ceramic tile.

C. Exterior stucco shall have integral color finish. Gypsum plaster shall have smooth trowel or sand float finish.

Section 09250: Gypsum Board Construction

A. Interior walls shall be gypsum board on 3½″ steel studs or furring.

B. Use ½″ thick board as standard, Fire Code Type X where required and moisture-resistant board at toilet rooms.

C. Core and Shaft Walls: Shall be manufacturer's UL-rated gypsum board and integral stud system.

Section 09300: Ceramic Tile

A. At floor of toilet rooms use 1″ × 1″ ceramic mosaic tile. At walls use 2″ × 2″ mosaic tile or 4″ × 4″ matte glazed ceramic tile.

B. Thin-set tile on concrete block; use organic adhesive on gypsum board; or full mortar bed on floors and walls where indicated. Grout and caulk with silicone sealant.

Section 09510: Acoustical Ceilings

A. Acoustical Tile: Use concealed spline system with 12″ × 12″ mineral fissured tile with access.

B. Suspension: Standard H or Z system.

OUTLINE SPECIFICATIONS Page 11 of

PROJECT IDENTIFICATION

Section 09650: Resilient Flooring

A. Floor tile, except storage rooms, toilets and janitor's closets, shall be ⅛″ vinyl-asbestos 12″ × 12″ tile equal to Kentile, Azrock, or Armstrong.

B. Provide 4″ vinyl-coved base in all areas with resilient flooring. At carpeted areas, base shall be straight type.

Section 09680: Carpeting

A. Carpet shall be 100 percent wool tufted velvet static protected and permanently mothproofed.

B. Padding shall be "Ozite" or equal 40-ounce hair felt.

C. Installation shall be by tackless strip method.

Section 09900: Painting

A. Exterior Metal:

One coat	Primer
Two coats	Low gloss exterior enamel

B. Gypsum Board:

One coat	Primer
Two coats	Latex

C. Interior Wood for Natural Finish:

Two coats	Penetrating sealer
One coat	Satin varnish

D. Interior Wood for Paint Finish:

One coat	Enamel undercoat
Two coats	Satin eggshell enamel

OUTLINE SPECIFICATIONS Page 12 of

PROJECT IDENTIFICATION

E. Interior Metal:

One Coat	Primer (or shop prime)
One Coat	Enamel undercoat
One coat	Satin eggshell enamel

Section 10000: Building Specialties

A. Electrically operated overhead doors.

B. Dock bumpers.

C. Trash compactor and trash chute.

D. Parking control equipment.

E. Lockers.

Section 10162: Metal Toilet Partitions

A. Floor-mounted pilaster-type, baked-enamel finish steel toilet partitions shall be used throughout including chrome-plated hardware with tamperproof screws.

B. Include toilet paper holders, coat hooks, etc.

C. Provide urinal screens where shown.

Section 11400: Food Service Equipment

A. Provide all food service equipment indicated.

B. Rough-in and final connection will be done under Mechanical and Electrical sections.

OUTLINE SPECIFICATIONS Page 13 of

PROJECT IDENTIFICATION

Section 11600: Laboratory Casework

A. Provide metal laboratory casework, including sinks and fittings furnished loose.

B. Tops shall be epoxy resin not less than 1¼″ thick.

C. Metal casework shall have chemical-resistant finish and base.

D. Fume Hoods: Shall have safety glazing and cement board linings. Interior of isotope hoods shall be stainless steel.

Section 13000: Special Construction

A. Standard prefabricated wood squash court.

B. Sauna construction and equipment.

C. Vault construction, including doors.

Section 14211: Electric Elevators

A. Type: Electric passenger elevator

B. Number: 2

C. Capacity: 1800 pounds

D. Platform Size: 5′-4″ wide × 4′-9″ deep outside

E. Speed: 175 feet per minute

F. Travel: 110′-0″ stopping at twelve (12) landings and serving twelve (12) openings

G. Power Supply: 208 volts, 3 phase, 60 cycles

H. Motors: 25 horsepower maximum

I. Operation: Duplex selective collective

OUTLINE SPECIFICATIONS Page 14 of

PROJECT IDENTIFICATION

J. Machine Room: Overhead

K. Doors: Two-speed, center-opening, field-painted

L. Cab: Standard cab with mat hooks, suspended ceiling, indirect lighting, enameled steel panels, stainless steel entrance columns, resilient flooring

M. Signals: Car position indicator at First Floor and in cab. Illuminated direction indicators at intermediate landings.

Section 15400: Plumbing

Section 15600: HVAC

Section 16000: Electrical Work

OUTLINE SPECIFICATIONS Page 15 of

Chapter Notes

Chapter 1: Formulating Master Outline Specifications

Page 3 ***MASTERFORMAT*** CSI document MP-2-1. Contains the sixteen divisions into which the project manual is organized, divided by trade and material. Standard numbers and titles are assigned to each section. This is the basic guide for all construction specifying. See also note on *Manual of Practice*, below.

Page 3 **CSI** The Construction Specifications Institute, "a nonprofit technical society of engineers, architects, contractors and others involved in the writing and interpretation of construction specifications." 601 Madison Street, Alexandria, Virginia 22314. Local chapters are active in most parts of the United States.

Page 4 **AIA SYSTEM** Use of the sixteen divisions with letters to differentiate sections, i.e., Section 9A, Painting. This method has been largely superseded now by the CSI all-digit system.

Page 4 **CSI SYSTEM** The all-digit preassigned numerical section identification set forth in *Masterformat*, i.e., Section 09900, Painting.

Page 4 ***MASTERSPEC*** The AIA master specification system offered by AIA Service Corporation, 1735 New York Avenue NW,

Washington, D.C. 20006. Designed to be edited, it includes notes and instructions to specifiers.

Page 4 **AIA** The American Institute of Architects, the United States architects' professional society, 1735 New York Avenue NW, Washington, D.C. 20006. Local chapters are active in most parts of the country.

Page 4 ***SPECTEXT*** "A library of coordinated master guide specification sections covering *Masterformat* divisions 1 through 16. Designed to be edited, it includes notes and instructions to specifiers."

Page 4 ***SECTION FORMAT*** CSI document MP-2-2 divides specification sections into three parts: Part 1, General Information; Part 2, Materials; Part 3, Installation.

Page 5 **ASTM** The American Society for Testing and Materials, 1916 Race Street, Philadelphia, Pa. 19103. Establishes tests and standards for materials. Publishes a comprehensive encyclopedia of standards annually. Heavily used as a specification reference.

Page 5 **ANSI** The American National Standards Institute, 1430 Broadway, New York, N.Y. 10018. Publishes and distributes agreed-on industry standards. Also serves as U.S. distributor for British Standards.

Page 5 **BUILDING SPECIALTIES** See Appendix C, Sample Outline Specification.

Chapter 2: Setting Bid Dates and Times

Page 8 **OFFSET REPRODUCTION** A photo-printing process extensively used for specification production. Its forgiving camera sufficiently masks the evidence of pasted-up originals to provide clean copies. Mainly used for large runs where electrostatic copying is less economical.

Page 9 **SEPARATE PRIME CONTRACTS** Under some jurisdictions certain contractors sign directly with the owner without the general contractor as intermediary. Usually used by government clients when required by statute.

Page 9 **FILED SUBBIDS** In Massachusetts public building contracts, selected subtrades bid directly to the awarding authority prior to receipt of general bids. Only a subbidder whose bid has been filed may be carried by general bidders in their lump-sum bids. This system makes prebid negotiations between general and subbidders difficult. A few other states have versions of this system as well.

Page 10 **STATUTORY BID OPENING** For example, in Massachusetts filed subbids are opened at noon in accordance with the statute. There is no such prescribed time for opening general bids, so the awarding authority sets the time.

Page 10 **SUBCONTRACTORS** Contractors for portions of the work, usually one trade each, who sign contracts with the general contractor for the work. When the owner pays the general contractor, appropriate portions of the payment are to be paid to the subcontractors by the general contractor.

Page 11 **BID BOND** A form of security usually provided by a third party (bondsman) guaranteeing that the bidder will contract to do the work at the price bid. The amount of the bond, commonly 5 to 10 percent of the bid, is forfeited to the owner should the bidder fail or refuse to sign the contract and is used then to offset the additional cost of selecting the second-lowest bidder at a higher price.

Page 12 **ADDENDA** See Chapter 10.

Page 12 **COMPETITIVE BIDDING** A system of determining construction cost involving submission of price proposals by several potential contractors based on contract drawings and specifications provided by the owner. Each bidder tries to submit the lowest price while demanding sufficient payment to accomplish the work profitably.

Chapter 3: Writing Consultants' Specifications

Page 15 **PROJECT MANUAL** The written portion of the contract documents, including bidding information and forms (if any), contract agreement, general conditions, and technical specifications.

Page 15 **CSI SECTION FORMAT** See notes for Chapter 1.

Page 15 **CSI SPECIFICATIONS COMPETITION** An annual judging of submitted project manuals from all parts of the United States with awards to those which conform in the best manner to CSI recommended practice. Winners are displayed at CSI's annual convention.

Page 16 **SUBMITTALS** Include shop drawings, manufacturers' data, record drawings, requests for changes and substitutions, samples of materials, etc.

Page 16 **CONSULTANTS** Typical consultants to the architect may include structural, electrical, plumbing, food service, site development, landscaping, civil engineering, medical equipment, acoustical, theatrical, lighting, energy conservation, etc.

Page 17 **GENERAL CONDITIONS** The legal framework of the construction contract which defines the duties and responsibilities of the parties and sets forth agreed-on procedures. Standard general conditions have been developed by AIA and the National Society of Professional Engineers (NSPE) in conjunction with the Associated General Contractors of America (AGC). Many of the clauses, written with extensive legal help, have been tested in court cases, so the exact wording is significant.

Page 17 **GENERAL REQUIREMENTS** Similar to the general conditions but more project-specific. They include sections on project meetings, temporary facilities, submittals, project administration, etc. General requirements are located in Division 1 of the project manual.

Chapter 4: The Well-Begun Project Manual

Page 19 ***MANUAL OF PRACTICE*** CSI's "basic guide providing theory, techniques, and formats for the organization of a construction project manual and the preparation of construction specifications. The complete *Manual of Practice* is composed of two volumes and supplementary documents.

"Volume I consists of 16 chapters offering guidance on the relationship of construction contract documents. It describes procedures and techniques for organizing, preparing and producing construction specifications and discusses the modification of architectural and engineering standard general conditions for various project conditions and for conformance with the CSI Format.

"Volume II consists of five chapters providing guidance and CSI formats for the subject organization and physical arrangement of specifications and their constituent parts. Volume II includes Masterformat: Master List of Specification Section Titles and Numbers." (Quoted from CSI *Newsdigest*, May 1984).

VOLUME I—Project Manual: Procedures and Techniques

- MP-1-1 Construction Documents and the Project Manual
- MP-1-2 Bidding Requirements
- MP-1-3 Types of Bidding and Contracts
- MP-1-4 The Agreement
- MP-1-5 Conditions of the Contract
- MP-1-6 Division 1—General Requirements
- MP-1-7 Relating Drawings and Specifications
- MP-1-8 Changes to Bidding and Contract Documents
- MP-1-9 Specification Writing and Production
- MP-1-10 Specifications Language
- MP-1-11 Methods of Specifying
- MP-1-12 Performance Specifications
- MP-1-13 Procurement Specifying
- MP-1-14 Civil Engineering Applications
- MP-1-15 Mechanical and Electrical Engineering Applications
- MP-1-16 Preparation and Use of an Office Master Specification.

VOLUME II—Formats: Specifications and Manuals

- MP-2-1 MASTERFORMAT: Master List of Section Titles and Numbers
- MP-2-2 SECTION FORMAT: Three-Part Section Format for Construction Specifications

MP-2-3 Page Format
MP-2-4 Performance Specifying Format
MP-2-5 Preparation of an Operation and Maintenance Manual

Page 19 **LUMP SUM, COST PLUS A FEE** Two types of owner-contractor agreements. Both use the same general conditions, AIA A-201. The first is AIA A-101, Standard Form of Agreement between Owner and Contractor for Use when the Basis of Payment Is a Stipulated Sum; the other is AIA A-111, Standard Form of Agreement between Owner and Contractor for Use when the Basis of Payment is the Cost of the Work Plus a Fee.

Page 20 **CSI *MASTERFORMAT*** See *Manual of Practice.*

Page 20 **SECTIONS** The basic unit of the project manual. Broad-scope sections may include more than one material or installation method. Narrow-scope sections generally deal with one product and its installation.

Page 20 **ALTERNATES** Separate items of work or separate parts of the project which the contractor is asked to price separately in the bid. The owner has the option to accept or reject alternates before signing the agreement. Each alternate must be clearly described and specified. Alternates involve work additional to the base bid or are decreases in the work required under the base bid.

Chapter 5: Bookkeeping

Page 23 **JOB TITLE** Each page of the project manual should have a unique job identification as well as a unique page number. If a page is found loose somewhere, it should be immediately identifiable. Job titles do not have to be exact or complete on each page but should be limited to about three words. Remember that you may do more than one project for the same owner. Using the office's job number for page identification is less satisfactory since it depends on each digit being accurate and readable. Using short names leaves less room for error and is often easier to remember.

Page 24 **ELECTRONIC EQUIPMENT** See Chapter 21.

Page 25 **DATE STAMPS** It's a good idea to get in the habit of date stamping all documents you receive: all product literature, letters, memos, regulations, progress prints, and such. The date of receipt is often valuable information years later—and not just in cases of litigation.

Chapter 6: From Manufacturer's Data into Specifications

Page 28 **CSI DATA** Obtainable from CSI national headquarters in Alexandria, Virginia. Members receive CSI *Newsdigest* monthly which contains a listing of all CSI publications and an order form. Nonmembers can also obtain documents directly.

Page 28 ***SPECDATA, MANUSPEC, TECHNICAL AIDS*** Quotations from James Sigel appeared in CSI *Newsdigest*, March 1980, page 8.

Chapter 7: Barrier-Free Specifications

Page 31 **ANSI A-117.1** Its title is: American National Standard Specification for Making Buildings and Facilities Accessible to and Usable by Physically Handicapped People.

Page 32 **DIVISIONS** The sixteen divisions of project manuals are listed in the index to the sample outline specification, Appendix C.

Chapter 8: Some Practical Aspects of Time Clauses

Page 36 **ESSENTIAL CONDITION CLAUSE** The example is taken from a typical U.S. government general conditions of a few years ago, HUD 4238-T, used in HUD's Academic Facilities program (9-66) and in many similar documents. The language of the clause has been tested in litigation and is not likely to change suddenly.

Page 39 **LIQUIDATED DAMAGES CLAUSE** Language taken from the same general conditions as the above. Both clauses are generally used together on government projects.

Page 42 **PROGRESS OF WORK CLAUSE** Typical clause from supplemental conditions used on private projects.

Chapter 9: Seven Sins of Specifying

Page 46 **RELATED WORK** Telling the reader of a trade's section what is *not* required is often very useful. Many specifiers use "Related Work Under Other Sections" to do this, without necessarily locating that other work precisely.

Page 46 **TRADE JURISDICTIONS** Often expressed in written agreements between affected unions. The union business agent can explain more quickly than you can read the legal prose in tiny print.

Page 50 **A-201** References in this book are to the thirteenth edition, August 1976. Current A-101 and A-111 are coordinated with this edition.

Page 50 **OSHA** The U.S. government's Occupational Safety and Health Act has wrought widespread and significant changes in manufacturing and construction during the last few years.

Chapter 11: Some Afterthoughts about Addenda

Page 56 **PAGE-BY-PAGE** Project manual page numbering is important for addenda references. A system of page numbering related to all-digit section identification, but which is still not clumsy when used in addenda, hasn't emerged so far.

Page 57 **THE *MANUAL OF PRACTICE* CONCEDES** Actually, the manual's earlier edition did concede this. The newest edition of MP-1-8 (1980) is silent on the matter, but it's still probably true.

Chapter 15: The "As-Built" Project Manual

Page 73 **AS-BUILT DRAWINGS** Insurors and lawyers caution against the architect's preparing or certifying drawings which claim to represent what was actually built (unless the architect was actually present and observed exactly what was done and where). In general, only the contractor is in a position to do this and to take responsibility for the accuracy of such drawings. The architect shouldn't get involved in liability for what has been done by others beyond normal contractual responsibility.

Page 74 **OR EQUAL** The familiar phrase added to a list of products which permits other similar products to be proposed for use. Used to set a standard and encourage price competition. See also Chapters 17 and 18.

Chapter 17: The Unique Product and the Public Bidding Laws

Page 83 **ALLOWANCES** A lump sum is carried by the contractor in the bid to cover the cost of an item whose value cannot be exactly determined at the time of bidding. Used for artwork, special finishes, and the like, or where final decisions haven't been made. If the cost of the material when purchased is less than the allowance, the balance is credited to the owner's account. If the cost is greater, the contractor is reimbursed for the additional amount.

Page 83 **"GOD IS IN THE DETAILS"** Commonly attributed to Ludwig Mies van der Rohe (1886–1970) known for his work on the Seagram building, New York City; Crown Hall at the Illinois Institute of Technology, Chicago; and the German Pavillion at the Barcelona Exposition of 1929 in Spain (now demolished).

Page 83 **CAESAR'S PROJECT MANUAL** With the above, a reference to the biblical statement: "Render therefore unto Caesar the things which are Caesar's; and unto God the things that are God's." *Matthew* 22:21

Chapter 19: Games Contractors Play

Page 91 **ADD-ONLY SUMS** For an example of this technique, see Appendix B.

Page 91 **CRITICAL PATH DIAGRAM** See Chapter 8.

Page 92 **CREDIT FOR DEFECTS NOT REMEDIED** See AIA A-201, paragraph 13.3.

Chapter 20: Games Owners Play

Page 93 **OWNER'S AGENT** See AIA A-201, paragraph 2.2.2.

Page 96 **CONSTRUCTION MANAGER** The types of construction management (CM) contracts are so varied and diverse that custom-tailored conditions are generally required to suit each case. Of course it's important that the contract conditions accurately reflect the type of arrangement the parties intend. CM is a relatively new endeavor and all the legal/contractual fallout hasn't settled yet.

Page 98 **JOE'S WINDOWS** A fictitious manufacturer.

Chapter 21: Stanford Revisited

Page 101 **THE STANFORD STUDY** "Automated Specifications—A Research Survey" published by the Construction Specifications Institute, Washington, D.C., November 1967.

Page 102 **STANFORD RESEARCH** CSI commissioned the Stanford Research Institute to perform the study.

Chapter 22: The Compleat Specifier

Page 107 — **PART 1** This chapter, being a specification for a specifier, is organized according to the CSI three-part section format. See MP-2-2.

Page 110 — **WHAT BELONGS ON DRAWINGS** Discussed in MP-1-7.

Chapter 23: Evaluating New Products

Page 112 — **NATIONAL BUREAU OF STANDARDS** Operates under the U.S. Department of Commerce, Gaithersburg, Maryland.

Page 112 — **INVERTED ROOF SYSTEMS** Popularly known as IRMA (inverted roof membrane assembly) places the waterproof membrane at the deck level with insulation, protection, and ballast above, as opposed to conventional roofing with the membrane on top of the insulation.

Page 113 — **ALEXANDER POPE** Prolific eighteenth-century poet (1688–1744). This verse is line 335 from his "Essay on Criticism" of 1711.

Chapter 26: Games Specifiers Play

Page 124 — **AWPA** The American Wood Preservers' Association, P.O. Box 849, Stevensville, Maryland, an industry association not to be confused with the AWPB, American Wood Preservers' Bureau, Box 6085, 2772 South Randolph Street, Arlington, Virginia, 22206 which operates a quality control laboratory and testing program, or the AWPI, American Wood Preservers' Institute, 1945 Gallows Road, Suite 405, Vienna, Virginia 22180, the promotional arm of the wood preservation industry. The three organizations are related.

Page 124 — **DIN** Deutsche Internationale Normen, the German standards, equivalent to our ASTM or British Standards. DIN standards are issued by the German Standards Organization, Deutsche Normenausschuss, Berlin.

Chapter 28: Specifier's Nightmare

Page 133 **STANFORD RESEARCH STUDY** See Chapter 21 and Appendix A.

Page 134 ***COMSPEC*** A standard system of handling information. *Comspec* is designed to handle any individual master specification electronically using time-shared computer facilities. User-generated documents or CSI *Spectext* masters can be used as a data base. Other master specifications are also available in this system.

Bibliography

Architects Handbook of Professional Practice, 2 volumes, American Institute of Architects, Washington, D.C. 1973, revised 1982. 21 chapters plus standard forms.

Building Contracts for Design and Construction, Harold D. Hauf, Wiley-Interscience, New York, 2d edition 1976.

Construction Specifications Handbook, Hans W. Meier, Prentice-Hall, Englewood Cliffs, N.J., 2d edition 1978.

Construction Specifications Writing, Harold J. Rosen, Wiley-Interscience, New York, 2d edition 1981.

Current Techniques in Architectural Practice, published jointly by American Institute of Architects, Washington, D.C., and Architectural Record/McGraw-Hill, New York, 1976. See Chapter 19, "Specifications," by Paul Heineman.

Library of Specifications Sections, Hans W. Meier, Prentice-Hall, Englewood Cliffs, N.J., 1983. 4 volumes, loose leaf.

Manual of Practice, Volume I—Project Manual: Procedures and Techniques, Construction Specifications Institute, Alexandria, Virginia, 1980. 16 chapters.

Manual of Practice, Volume II—Formats: Specifications and Manuals, Construction Specifications Institute, Alexandria, Virginia, 1983. 5 chapters. Includes Masterformat, master list of section titles and numbers, which can also be purchased separately as document MP-2-1.

Principles of Specification Writing, Harold J. Rosen, Reinhold, New York, 1967.

Specifications for Architecture, Engineering and Construction, Chesley Ayers, McGraw-Hill, New York, 2d edition 1984.

index

Page numbers in *italic* indicate chapter notes.

about the author

Walter Rosenfeld did his undergraduate work at the University of Pennsylvania and studied architecture at Yale. He has been a registered architect for almost 20 years and holds an NCARB certificate. He joined the Construction Specifications Institute in 1967 and is a certified construction specifier as well as a Director of CSI's Boston chapter. He has won several awards in CSI's annual specifications competitions. His specifications for major buildings include the Johns-Manville World Headquarters near Denver, Colorado; the Shawmut Bank office building in Boston; and the AIA Headquarters in Washington, DC. For over 12 years he was head of the Specifications Department at The Architects Collaborative (TAC) in Cambridge, Massachusetts, where he authored that organization's master specifications and pioneered in automating the company's specifications production. He is currently a principal of the firm.

In addition, he serves as a Contributing Editor to *Progressive Architecture* and writes regularly on specifications subjects.

DATE DUE

FEB. 28 1990
MAR. 27 1990
JUL. 14 1993
APR 27 '95
APR. 29 2002
SEP 27 2006
AUG 04 2008
AUG 04 2009

GAYLORD PRINTED IN U.S.A.